W9-DES-912

The Fruitful Darkness

ALSO BY JOAN HALIFAX

The Human Encounter with Death
(with Stanislav Grof)

Shamanic Voices

Shaman: The Wounded Healer

The Fruitful Darkness

RECONNECTING WITH THE
BODY OF THE EARTH

Joan Halifax

HarperSanFrancisco
A Division of HarperCollins*Publishers*

Copyright credits begin on page 237.

Harper San Francisco and the author, in associa-
tion with the Rainforest Action Network, will facilitate the planting of two trees for every one
tree used in the manufacture of this book.

THE FRUITFUL DARKNESS. *Reconnecting with the Body of
the Earth.* Copyright © 1993 by Joan Halifax. All rights
reserved. Printed in the United States of America. No
part of this book may be used or reproduced in any
manner whatsoever without written permission except
in the case of brief quotations embodied in critical
articles and reviews. For information address
HarperCollins Publishers, 10 East 53rd Street,
New York, NY 10022.

ILLUSTRATIONS BY KATHERINE TILLOTSON

FIRST HARPERCOLLINS PAPERBACK EDITION
PUBLISHED IN 1994.

ISBN 0–06–250313–8 (pbk.)

An Earlier Edition of This Book Was Cataloged As Follows:
Halifax, Joan.
 The fruitful darkness : reconnecting with the body
of the earth / Joan Halifax. — 1st ed.
  p. cm.
 Includes bibliographical references.
 ISBN 0–06–250369–3 (alk. paper)
 1. Spiritual life. 2. Earth—Religious aspects. 3.
Shamanism. 4. Spiritual life—Buddhism.
 I. Title
 BL624.H35 1993
 291.4'2—dc20   92–53905

---

94 95 96 97 98 ❖ RRD(H) 10 9 8 7 6 5 4 3 2 1

This edition is printed on acid-free paper that meets the
American National Standards Institute
Z39.48 Standard.

Benedicto: May your trails be crooked,
   winding, lonesome,
dangerous, leading to the most amazing
   view.
May your rivers flow without end,
meandering through pastoral valleys
   tinkling with bells,
past temples and castles and poets' towers
into a dark primeval forest where tigers
   belch and monkeys howl,
through miasmal and mysterious swamps
   and down into a desert of red rock,
blue mesas, domes and pinnacles and
   grottos of endless stone,
and down again into a deep vast ancient
   unknown chasm
where bars of sunlight blaze on profiled
   cliffs,
where deer walk across the white sand
   beaches,
where storms come and go
as lightning clangs upon the high crags,
where something strange and more beautiful
and more full of wonder than your deepest
   dreams
waits for you—
beyond the next turning of the canyon
   walls.

                              —Edward Abbey

Contents

Acknowledgments

This writing is an expression of gratitude to those men and women who helped me weave my way back into the fabric of Earth. As I write, I want to remember Dolo Ogobara, Don José Ríos (Matsuwa), Guadalupe de la Cruz Ríos, Maria Sabina, Chan K'in Viejo, Jorge K'in, Don Tomas, Grandfather Telles Goodmorning, Grandfather Semu Huaute, Grandfather Wallace Black Elk, Grandmother Grace Spotted Eagle, Grandmother Caroline Tawangyawma, James Kootshongsie, Grandfather Leon Shenandoah, Gray Whiskers, Joe David, John Goodwin (Nytom), Nico Dzib, and other native peoples who have tried patiently to help me see how we live intimately with and within each other.

I also want to remember the Buddhist teachers who showed me the truth of interconnectedness and compassion, including Dae Soen sa Nim, Chakdud Tulku Rinpoche, Richard Baker Roshi, Cao Ngoc Phuong, and my root teacher, Thich Nhat Hanh. And I want to confirm the gifts from the many friends who traveled with me to wild lands of person and place, people who have entered the fruitful darkness with me. This darkness and gold is the heart of the teaching of all these companions and teachers of the way.

I am also writing both to and from the spirit of the wilderness. It used to be that human beings and the wilderness could not be separated. For tens of thousands of years, one has been a context for the other. Today, in North America anyway,

ix

wilderness is not the homeland and place of renewal for primal peoples but a place where people of industrial cultures go for "recreation." Yes, there is still wilderness in America—both big and small, and its survival is our survival.

Like many of you, I have traveled a long way to find a bit of true nature. Yet it exists in intimate forms all around us—in the mushroom that pushes its white head through a crack in the asphalt, in the rich collection of so-called weeds that find their way to water along the roads of New Mexico. Wilderness can be seen from the top floor of Rockefeller Plaza as the peregrine falcon flies by. Wilderness lives in the hedges around Miami's shopping malls, which are a commons for bird and bee. Wilderness is the wood rat whose big old nest is tucked into sage in the oak groves in Ojai, in the coyote who finds a den in the brush of Beverly Hills, in the chipmunk who steals seed from the bird feeder for her winter supply in the Appalachian fall of North Carolina. We look quietly to see these expressions of the wilds all around us.

Wilderness lives within us as well—in the beating of our blood, in the wild root of our imagination. As I write, I remember this skin wrapping around my animal body as it shook uncontrollably when I found myself hanging to a thin lip of granite on a rock face in Baja. This body that exhausted and exalted itself on the Dolma Pass of Mount Kailas. This body that was covered with friendly bruises after swimming with rough, playful dolphins. This body whose lungs strained for a little more oxygen as I walked to Dudh Kund. I remember hair standing on end in rain forests and temperate forests and in northern waters when I encountered creatures, like jaguar and orca, who were higher on the food chain. This, all of it, is Earth's true nature, including the mind that lives through this body and Earth.

I bow in gratitude to:

Traveling companions Paul Adams, Steve Brown, Diane Bunting and Loren White, Gigi Coyle, Daku Tenzing Norgay, Barrett Eagle Bear, Dana Fonte, Verona Halifax Fonte, Brother John, Cynthia Jurs, John Madison, Jim Nollman, Joan and Barry Norris, Robert Ott, Lola Rae, Ted Joans, Hans Van de Bovenkamp, the late John Watts, Andy and Sabina Weil, and Nina Wise;

Teachers and colleagues Mary Catherine Bateson, the late Joseph Campbell, Bill Devall, Steven Foster and Meredith Little, Peter Furst, Stanislav Grof, Alan Lomax, James Lovelock, Joanna Macy, the late Margaret Mead, the late Barbara Myerhoff, John Weir Perry, Richard Evans Schultes, William Irwin Thompson, Francisco Varela, the late Gordon Wasson, and Johannes Wilbert;

Valued editorial advisers Tom Grady, Katinka Matson, Caroline Pincus, Marilyn Preston, Kazuaki Tanahashi, Miriam Bobkoff, and most especially Michael Gruber and Frances Harwood;

And source of great inspiration and support: Laurance S. Rockefeller, and my beloved parents, John Halifax and the late Eunice Halifax.

Foreword

Out of suffering, compassion may be born. Compassion is the balm that refreshes and heals us and brings back our smile. *The Fruitful Darkness* is a journey of suffering and compassion. Joan Halifax, our friend, guide, and teacher, leads us on this important adventure. With her guidance, we are able to see more deeply into ourselves—into our true nature and the true nature of the mountains, rivers, skies, Earth, and all living beings. And we can see the beauty of all that is—the beauty in us, the beauty of an autumn leaf floating to the ground, the beauty of a snail crossing our path. Beauty can be found in birth and also in dying. If we know how to live, we will also know how to die. Living in beauty means dying in beauty. The deepest way to be alive and the deepest way to die are the same—doing so in harmony with everyone and everything, in the true spirit of interbeing. The moment we do this, ideas of self and nonself, life and death, vanish, and we experience joy, equanimity, and nonfear.

Suffering is sometimes unavoidable, and when we must suffer, we can accept it, with compassion. Eighty-four thousand doors open to the truth of interbeing, and suffering is one of them. But there are also other doors, including joy and loving-kindness. Joan opens so many doors for us. I am grateful to her for writing this book.

Thich Nhat Hanh
Plum Village, Duras, France
July 1992

The tao that can be told
is not the eternal Tao.
The name that can be named
is not the eternal Name.
The unnameable is the eternally real.
Naming is the origin
of all particular things.
Free from desire, you realize the mystery.
Caught in desire, you see only the manifes-
tations.
Yet mystery and manifestations
arise from the same source.
This source is called darkness.
Darkness within darkness.
The gateway to all understanding.

Lao-tzu, translated by
Stephen Mitchell

Preface

I take refuge in Buddha's body
   Christ's body
   Earth's body
   Sky's body
I take refuge in the truth of abiding and changing
I take refuge in the four worlds
   of combining elements
   of giving plants
   of creatures
   and two-leggeds—
all companions in awakening

Writing in landscapes, landscapes write in you. Sending a voice to the Juarez Mountains of Baja, the Sangre de Cristos of Colorado, the Blue Ridge Mountains of North Carolina, the Himalayas; sending a voice to Death Valley, Ojai Valley, and the hills and valleys of France's Dordogne; sending a voice to the changeable waters of the Virgin Islands and the cold, radiant waters of Tibet's Lake Manasaraovar; sending a voice to Mexico's wet lowland forests and Canada's dark stands of cedar; sending a voice to Abiquiu and the Chama, to Yaxchilán and the Usumacinta. Sending a voice. Yes, it is true; each place has its own voice. Sending a voice, a voice responds.

Thus it is with Earth. From the silence, from the space and place empty of society, in the land, in the sea, and the beings that abide within these living forms, and in the great atmosphere that holds the Earth's body can be heard the voices of ancestors, elements and elementals, plants and creatures, the roar of water and ice, the whisper and whistle of pine, the swoosh of the hawk, the song of the eagle. The voice of nature can be heard.

Nature's voice can be also heard in the city, on the highway, in airports and in slums, in hospitals and schools, in Disneyland and shopping malls. The weave of nature excludes nothing from its fabric, not even the crazy and destructive, creative and inspiring ideas of human beings.

I have known this since I was a child, first discovering this truth during a period of blindness and paralysis at the age of four when I fell ill with a grave virus—a time of darkness, a time to dream. As I matured, I went into outer and inner wilderness to remember the continuum of which I am a part. I could not know it with my conceptual mind. Learning came through my body, with my flesh—my eyes, ears, nose, tongue, and body—touching the body of Earth. Dualism is so strongly embedded in industrial culture that I had to leave this culture to reaffirm the truth of nonduality, that we are all on this great distributive lattice together.

Over years of travel, study, and practice, I have seen the destruction of wild environments, the suffering of indigenous peoples at the hands of industrialized peoples, and the loss of a view of life as sacred. All this has turned me and many others to non-Western traditions as a way of understanding the nature of our own aggression toward and alienation from Earth. Some have sought understanding in Eastern traditions; others, the way of the Sufi or Celtic mysteries. Many have explored the world of primal peoples who form part of the Paleolithic continuity. Others have expanded the view of their root religions. Still others have used psychology, anthropology, physics, biology, ecology, feminism, and wilderness as ways to see themselves in the nature of the world. I myself entered the stream of Buddhist practice and shamanism as a basis for exploring mind and Earth, suffering and compassion.

I, like many others, sought fresh answers in ancient fields, not only in the old Ways of elder cultures, East and West, but in old forests and old river bodies. I looked for root-truth in language, in food, in social institutions, and in mind itself, what one Lakota elder calls "the root that has no end." This self that is coextensive with all of creation holds within it the sense of a continuum as vast as the oceans flowing around Earth. Where is the end? Where is the beginning? And so it is with the story of Earth, or the stories recounted in this book, or even the story of one's own life. The thread of cause and effect can be followed endlessly as it weaves a whole cloth.

Although the cloth of this book reflects the years I spent studying anthropology, psychology, and mythology as well as practicing Buddhism and shamanism and living with wilderness and with tribal peoples, my part in this story begins not in the wild mountains of Asia or the rain forests of Mexico but in the concrete canyons of

New York in the mid-1960s. Like many young people of that era, I worked for the civil rights of black people in the United States and was active against the tragic war in Vietnam. In that world of protesting physicists and playwrights, academicians and students, I met the anthropologist Alan Lomax, who was doing a cross-cultural analysis of song and dance style. I joined his research project at Columbia University and for four years listened to music from all over the world.

Sitting in the tape archives at Columbia, I was convinced that the planet still held many secrets, many refuges. Although I was aware that indigenous peoples across the Earth had suffered profoundly and that many elder cultures were no longer viable, I was, like most North Americans, naive; I did not realize the extent to which the natural environments and lifeways of tribal people had been eroded and, in many instances, extinguished by the fear and greed of peoples in dominating nations. Yes, the tenacity of these old traditions has protected some of them from complete extinction. They live on in trailer parks, in urban slums, or in corners of remote wilderness. Others are enjoying a revival, like the renaissance of traditional life among some peoples of the Northwest Coast. But still, the Earth that all of us live on today is vastly changed from the Earth of the recent ancestors of tribal peoples.

The planet seems much smaller, more interconnected, and more vulnerable to me these days. Human economies and environmental systems, from the World Bank to Brazilian rain forests, are intimately related. We can see clearly now how human actions affect all life on Earth. In two days we can travel from Los Angeles, New York, or London to the heart of what is left of the Lacandon rain forest in southern Mexico. We can visit with the old Lacandon shaman Chan K'in Viejo and listen to him speak about the body of our world:

> What the people of the city do not realize is that the roots of all living things are tied together. When a mighty tree is felled, a star falls from the sky. Before one chops down a mahogany, one should ask permission of the guardian of the forest, and one should ask permission of the guardian of the stars. Hachäkyum made the trees, and he also made the stars, and he made them from the same sand and clay, ashes and lime. When the great trees are cut down, the rain ends, and the forest turns to weed and grass. . . . There is too much cold in the world now, and it has worked its way into the hearts of all living creatures and down into the roots of the grass and the trees. But I am not afraid. What saddens me is that I must live to see the felling of the trees and the drying up of the forest, so that all the animals die, one after the other, and only the snakes live and thrive in the thickets.

Interestingly, these thickets are where the possibility for the future lives, and we meet now in this rough and dangerous boundary land between old and new, the past and the future. It is here that we still find some of the old wisdom of tribal peoples: how they felt and feel about the Earth; how our star and other stars line out a choreography of hunting, gathering, planting, and praying; how the passing of the moons and the coming and going of plants and creatures shape a living calendar; how prophecy protects the future and myth instructs the present; how for many peoples, one's relations are confirmed not only by bloodlines but also by song-lines; how all is perceived as being alive, each landscape filled with power and song.

In the late sixties, I left New York and Columbia University for France, to work at the Musée de l'Homme in Paris to prepare myself for a visit to the Dogon people of Mali in central Africa. I spent part of 1970 with the Dogon, where I witnessed the Sigui, a rite of passage for the culture and a ritual of renewal for the land itself. It was with the Dogon that I realized how culturally impoverished we are with respect to ritual process and rites of passage. While there, I kept asking myself, How can we renew ourselves personally and culturally? Where are the threshold rites that mark living and dying, mourning and marriage, birth and childhood, vision and darkness? What are the consequences of living in a world that prevents us from knowing directly the season's change, the planting and harvesting of our food, the births and deaths of our loved ones? Where are the rites that renew our relationship with Earth? How can we enter the darkness of self and psyche and retrieve the fruits of compassion from our suffering?

Dolo Ogobara, the Dogon who helped me to understand the ways of his people, used to say to me as we were walking across the scorching Bandiagara cliffs, *"Petit pas, Jeanne"* (Little steps, Joan). His was a world where the human touch, the world of culture, was a way to express the fine order of the cosmos. His was a world that renewed itself in rites of birth and reversal that freed one from the staleness of forgetting. The missionaries had burned the wooden images of the gods of the Dogon, but the power of the Earth, the power of the sky prevailed in the Dogon's patterns of sanity and trueness.

I walked behind Ogobara in his pale sand-colored homespun robes on many miles of desert and rock, through cool caves that were home to vipers, down steep gold cliffs into the shrines, homes, and granaries of his people. These architectural structures, like the drum rhythms heard during ceremonial times, held the patterns of a life in order.

I understood that Ogobara's admonishment for me to take little steps involved more than walking across the hot Bandiagara cliff tops. Like most Westerners, I wanted to take giant steps, even to skip steps. But he kept me taking one little step at a time, lest I be presumptuous, lest I hurt myself, lest I hurt others. It is clear to me that his admonishment was also literal. He wanted me to take little, careful steps as I made my way across the great expanse of high rock in Dogon land. That is how his people did it.

Years later, when I practiced walking meditation with my Buddhist teacher Thich Nhat Hanh, I found myself walking at the same pace, with the same expanded concentration and appreciation for the land. Both then and now, when I walk mindfully with "little steps," my breath and body remember Ogobara and the confidence of a life lived in the truth of its continuity with both time and space.

One day I was to leave this desert world of tiny millet fields, giant water gourds, and dark shining faces. Though ill with liver disease, I wanted to weave a new cloth in my life and the life of my culture. I was not of the same flesh as the one who had traveled across the Sahara to the Dogon. My feet were hard from long walking. My face was creased and dark from the sun. My body was lean and alive, not the weary New York flesh of my early twenties.

I had also discovered new flesh in my mind. Long stretches of timespace in the solitudes of the desert, long periods in the quiet depths of an endless landscape and a great horizon, stepping into forbidden zones where ancestors were buried—and being forgiven—being tutored by the old man in the ancestral teachings of those who had gone before him, seeing how the heavenly bodies (even invisible ones) drew on the life waters even in this dry landscape, seeing the tracks of the mythical white fox across the diviner's map inscribed in the desert floor, in all these I felt the signs of unseen patterns becoming visible, of dreaming made real.

I too wanted to make the dream real, or to know what was real, what was true. Here, far from my homeland, the hidden patterns of my culture were becoming visible. I was filled with questions as I lived between the culture of my birth and the culture of the Dogon. These questions are the keys that have unlocked some of the rooms I explore in this book.

I withdrew slowly and reluctantly from this African world. I had contracted hepatitis when I traveled to Senegal to pick up supplies. Returning to the Dogon, I saw that it was time to leave Africa. Between the war in Chad, my depleted physical condition, and not wanting to leave my friends of the Sahel, the journey back to my family in southern Florida was protracted. I had found a home in this old spacious world of sky and desert and did not want to return to the West. The world I had come from—New York, Miami, North Carolina—looked quite disordered as I sat in the quiet shadow of the cliffs above Banani, but I eventually realized that most of us have to return to the world from which we started.

After a recovery of several months, I went to work as a medical anthropologist at the University of Miami School of Medicine. Miami was a gateway for refugees and migrant workers from the Caribbean and Latin America. Here was a place where old Africa and old Spain met with the new West. I learned to be a "cultural broker," building bridges between the conventional medical system and the healing systems of the local community, in which *santeros, espiritistas,* root doctors, and other local healers offered their services.

There were no expansive deserts in Miami but an abundance of highways, condominiums, housing projects, and decaying shacks. Here refugees from the Caribbean and Latin America were trying to make sense of a fragmented world. In the confusion of cultural change, Cubans renewed themselves in their *cabildos,* Haitians danced their gods, and the small storefront Christian churches in Coconut Grove were filled every night of the week.

My world had shifted radically when I left New York and Paris for Africa. From cross-cultural studies in archives to fieldwork in Africa and the Dogon's great rite of passage, the Sigui, I switched from mind to body. My world was again to shift, this time from body to psyche, when I married the psychiatrist Stanislav Grof. I left Miami and went to work with him at the Maryland Psychiatric Research Center on his project of LSD-assisted psychotherapy with people dying of cancer. Here was a contemporary rite of passage for people immediately facing death. For the first time, I was no longer an observer of a rite of passage but part of the action, working with people who were actually on the threshold between life and death.

During my years with Grof, I often pondered the question of who is really prepared to be with the dying. Certainly, at the age of thirty, I had little to offer but my presence to most of the people with whom I worked. At times this work was a terrible trial for me. Not only were the cancer patients suffering, but my own life was beginning to unravel. I was about to join the list of casualties of Western culture as I plunged into the depths of mental and physical confusion. I felt real compassion for those dying of cancer. I was convinced that I too was losing my life; a lump in my breast and excessive uterine bleeding convinced me I had cancer. During this period of physical illness, I was also suffering extreme mental anguish. Nothing in Western culture seemed to help me, from psychotherapy to modern pharmacology.

In the climax of this psychomental crisis, Grof and I divorced. The fabric of my life had unraveled completely. Groundless, I turned toward the dharma and the empty loom of Buddhism when I began to practice with a *sangha* (community) and the Korean Zen Master Dae Soen sa Nim. I also plunged into an intense exploration of plant teachers, such as peyote, and went to Mexico to visit Huichol peoples, who used this hallucinogenic cactus as a sacrament. With the Huichols, I was to leap across a cultural chasm and a personal one as well. Like Ogobara in Africa, the Huichol shaman Don José Ríos was to guide me through an unknown but spacious territory that for me was physically and mentally renewing and that eventually returned me to health and humor.

The flower of the mind would bloom in various and strange ways as I took this inspiration back to New York, where I did research for Joseph Campbell on *The Way of the Animal Powers*. While working for Campbell, I continued to travel to Mexico and explore the territories of the plant teachers with Don José and his family and with Mazatec friends, including the healer Maria Sabina.

One morning, I told Joe the following dream: I am in a longhouse of native peoples of Canada. I look out the door and see to the west a great circle of men and women from all races and all nations sitting on a meadow of brilliant green. I go to join them, and as I approach, I rise into the air. I am at first afraid and incredibly self-conscious, but soon others join me. I awaken ecstatic.

Although I was pretty happy about the dream, Joe said to me, "Joan, you should put pennies in your shoes." I asked him what he meant, and he replied evenly that I seemed a bit "out there." Indeed I had seriously overextended myself both physically and psychologically. I wanted to know about mind and its potential in as many ways as possible. Mythology, anthropology, and psychology were points of departure. I had felt compelled to go further afield, into shamanism, and into tribal cultures that used psychoactive plants in their shamanic practices. I also yearned to be in the mountains, in the wilderness, away from the omnipresent hum of Western culture.

Joe, in fact, was being more than polite when he recommended that I "put pennies in my shoes." Though I felt that I was exploring the edge, Campbell was convinced that I had gone over it. He was right. I needed to get out of the mindstuff that took me upward. I needed to get out of the high rises of New York and the highs of psychoactive plants. I needed to get down to Earth. I needed the big views of the mountains without the "visionary vegetables." Later I would understand that magic lives in the so-called ordinary world, in the details of our everyday lives. It is in these simple moments that we can really appreciate the magic of this world. When Buddha realized enlightenment, he touched the Earth. This gesture connected him to the world; it made him the world's relation. I needed to "touch the Earth."

In the late 1970s, I took Joe's advice and moved to Ojai, California, to "touch the Earth" or, to put it more accurately, to be touched by it. I began an educational community called the Ojai Foundation. Buddhist practice and the wilderness became the antidote to the intellectual and visionary worlds that were consuming me. At Ojai, I tried to replicate the experience of intimacy with place that I had known with Ogobara, Don José, and other tribal peoples. I wanted to live as close to the Earth as possible. I also wanted to create a place where people from various cultures and traditions could meet together and exchange with one another in an environment that was sacred, friendly, and wild.

Ojai was a refuge where shamanism and Buddhism interacted in an earthy way. Our largest classroom and meditation space was under an immense old oak tree whose great crown sheltered us from the sun. There were shrines where people left offerings, paths through the forest for walking meditation, a large organic garden that became home to different species of creatures and plants. And along with daily meditation practice there were nightly gatherings around a small fire in the kiva. There also arose the predictable organizational and financial strains in establishing an educational community with a spiritual base, as well as psychosocial challenges one might expect when meditation, psychological work, community process, and service to others are combined in the practice of daily life.

Because of the complex experience at Ojai, I entered the body of Buddhist practice with greater commitment. My continuing visits with Don José and other shamans and Buddhist teachers from traditional societies—old men and women from the rain forests of Mexico to the high plateau of Tibet—would keep turning my mind back to Earth and help me weave my life more tightly into its fabric.

Over the twelve years at Ojai, I extended my investigations of Buddhism and shamanism by traveling to Buddhist areas, including Tibet, Ladakh, Zanskar, Sikkim, Bhutan, and Sherpa and Gurung areas of Nepal. The mountains and their peoples were instrumental in shaping my body and mind. They humbled me, brought me down and in, as I walked in their midst. The mountains, I would discover, were protectors and teachers who relentlessly taught me about the authority of stillness as I moved among them. I needed their authority. I needed their strength; I needed their transcendent endurance. The simple act of walking, I learned, was initiation.

Studying shamanism, entering the deep wilderness of mountain, forest, and desert, as well as living in Ojai's semiwilderness, I realized that I was learning about a psychological zone that existed not only inside the forest dweller but inside me as well. It was not a matter of including the "primitive" into my world but of recognizing these archaic elements in my very nature. This contact with indigenous peoples and the wilds had transformed my physical body, my mind, and my relationship to Earth. Ojai was a place where I (as well as others) could explore this real but rarely understood territory.

Although I had taken the first five Buddhist vows to not harm in the mid-seventies, the Buddhist stream would widen and deepen for me when in the early spring of 1985, I met the Vietnamese monk Thich Nhat Hanh. The scale of my life shifted as Buddhism became a way to practice intimacy with the world. Rooted in the utter practicality of nonviolence, Buddhist practice and teaching since the sixties had strongly influenced my life and my way of thinking. Through Thich Nhat Hanh's example and guidance, practice became warm and relaxed, at its base nonviolent and nondenying. Also through this new way of practice, I came to know the true value of fully facing my own suffering and the suffering of other beings.

◢ ◣ ◢

The Fruitful Darkness is in part the story of the journey that took me through an encounter between the body of Buddhist practice and the body of tribal wisdom, especially shamanism. "Our own life is the instrument with which we experiment with Truth," wrote Thich Nhat Hanh. This book is a description of such an experiment. It is grounded in direct experience, practice, and intuition. My personal experiences are the main source for the text; the information and inspiration in this book are rooted in my life. This is inevitable, for neither Buddhism nor shamanism are "revealed" teachings. Both emphasize direct experience and personal realization over doctrine. In my years of practicing, working, and living with these traditions, I have discovered the profound value of truth that is directly known, directly understood, directly realized.

The book is also about the practice of ecology, an ecology of mind and spirit in relation to the Earth, an ecology that sees initiation as a way of reconciling self and other, an ecology that confirms the yield of the darkness, the fruit of suffering, an ecology of compassion.

Like Buddhism and shamanism, deep ecology is centered on questioning and directly understanding our place from within the web of creation. All three of these practices—Buddhism, shamanism, and deep ecology—are based on the experience of engagement and the mystery of participation. Rooted in the practice and art of compassion, they move from speculation to revelation through the body of actual experience.

There are many roads into the territory of nonduality. I have chosen to reflect on those that I have traveled. What follows are observations, notes, stories, and realizations that point to pathways that link self and other—ways that often take one through the Valley of Darkness. I also suggest that the fruits of understanding and compassion grow in this Valley.

I have lived on the lip
of insanity, wanting to know reasons,
knocking on a door. It opens.
I've been knocking from the inside!

Rumi, translated by Coleman Barks
with John Moyne

1

The World Wound

We know ourselves to be made from this earth.
We know this earth is made from our bodies.
For we see ourselves. And we are nature. We
are nature seeing nature. We are nature with a
concept of nature. Nature weeping. Nature
speaking of nature to nature.

Susan Griffin, *Woman and Nature*

In the fall of 1990, I sat in a wash high above
Owens Lake, now a desiccated pallet of pale,
shifting color. Owens Valley stretches its long
open body east of the Sierra Nevada in California.
In its middle is the alkali floor of what was once
an immense river-fed lake used by steamboats to
transport salt from the Saline Valley and silver
from the Inyos. Now great clouds of gray dust
blow in the four directions from its basin, emptied in the early 1900s by the water lords of Los
Angeles.

Close companions were fasting in the rugged
canyons branching off from the rocky depression
where we had made a base camp. These friends
were taking refuge in silence and solitude. It was a
time for them to separate themselves from their
everyday lives, a time they had given to themselves to mark change in their lives, as people of

many cultures have done, to renew their relationship with creation. Each spring for years, I too have gone into wilderness alone to fast, to empty and restore myself. Now, however, I was to "bear witness" for my friends. With teachers Steven Foster and Meredith Little, I would pray for these men and women as they went out, each one alone, without food or shelter, into this seemingly empty terrain.

Sitting in the rocky, windy land, my mind turned to Los Angeles, the vast city to the south that had sucked Owens Valley dry. Thousands of dead trees stand as silent witnesses to the destruction. The skies also witness this changing time with drought. Deer have retreated far into the higher reaches of the Sierra, and hunters complain. Old-timers around these parts say even the snakes are dying out for lack of water.

On our first afternoon in the south Inyo Mountains ("Dwelling Place of a Great Spirit") before people left for their fasts, the heavens were roaring with the sound of fighter planes training for our nation's most recent war. They were so close we could see the missiles clinging to their wings like dark lampreys. I wondered if the military would play war games all weekend, or would we have quiet instead, in this big, rugged commons? The human fingerprint is found today in every drop of rain. Is there any place on Earth where the voice of technology is not heard?

Early the next morning, my friends left in an unexpected rainstorm for their lonely vigils in the bare mountains just to the north. For most of the day and throughout the night rain raced in all directions. Usually, rain makes me smile. When I was growing up in Florida and North Carolina, bad weather meant rain. But I lived for twelve years in Southern California, and bad weather in California during the seventies and eighties meant *no* rain. I wondered what the rain would do for my fasting friends. How would it affect their internal weather?

I have always loved the smell of rain in the desert, with the bitter-fresh smell of ozone impregnating the atmosphere. The old, dry sage plants resurrect with rain. The rocks seem to give off a perfume as they show their true colors. The desert floor changes its contours before your very eyes. I still listen with interest to the voices of rain, sometimes harsh and driving, sometimes lyrical.

In the midst of this horizontal rain, I bedded down in the back of a covered pickup and listened till sleep came. At dawn, high and dry, I enjoyed the view of the drenched desert, waking up to light on the surface of each stone and pebble. After sunrise, a bright rainbow tied the world together. Then followed the silence of a cloudless day.

Silence makes the secretions of the mind visible. At first my "mental secretions" took the predictable form of an analysis of the "decline of the West" as well as everything else. East and West, North and South are a continuum, I reminded myself. The Paleolithic continuity, the world of tribal peoples, the wilderness they lived in, and dead Owens Lake are not separate and distinct from Los Angeles and Las Vegas. By emptying myself when I fast, emptying myself in solitude, I might discover myself full—of history, wilderness, and society. And I can see my identity co-evolving with all of creation. I reminded myself as I watched the clouds collecting over the Sierra that we don't know the end of this story. The current state of events, however, had left little doubt in my mind about how pervasive suffering is in creation's continuum.

After these ruminations, I began to look around me at a rugged "unromantic" landscape—no flashy red rock twisted by the wind, no mushroom-shaped stones, no flower-filled meadows or lush forests, just scree, gray washes, and ragged mountains. This land would probably not induce visionary inflation in the fasters, I thought. Yet its beauty was subtle, with worn rock, bits of obsidian flakes from former inhabitants, a flash of pale pink in the cut or turn of a canyon. Yet most people would call this a wasteland.

When we first entered the area, I had to look hard to see where my friends might put themselves; there seemed to be nothing here. But on a second look, I could see the shadows of Earth where it turned upon itself, hiding places to take refuge from sun, wind, and rain. I was satisfied with this secretive environment; no one would bother to come here except a few hungry fools.

As a Western woman, whatever I have learned about the nature of the self, both the local and the extended self, has been by going inward and down into the fruitful darkness, the darkness of culture, the darkness of psyche, the darkness of nature. The most important secrets seem always to hide in the shadows. "The secret of life," say the Utes, "is in the shadows and not in the open sun; to see anything at all, you must look deeply into the shadow of a living thing."

I have entered this shadow world mostly unwillingly. Having found the gold of compassion in the dark stone of suffering, having tasted the fruit of sanity in the tangled grove of the self, I also willingly entered the Valley of the Shadow through solitude, silence, stillness, meditation, and prayer. In those quiet places I discovered a mindstream whose depths were luminous.

The third morning in Owens Valley, Steven swore that something or someone had come to camp in the early hours. I walked around camp, checking the kitchen and vehicles, and all looked quite normal to me. Steven made coffee, and we settled into a good talk as we waited for Meredith to return from town.

A little after nine, she arrived. I could see from a distance that her face was tight with concern. Steven saw it as well, and he approached the car quietly. It was she who bore the news that my mother had died unexpectedly that morning.

The first thing that I could see was my mother's face, a face that had always turned away from her own suffering even as she faced the suffering of others. Her life had been one of service. As a tall and beautiful woman in her twenties, she had mastered the craft of making books for the blind. And I was to learn later that on the last day of her life, twelve hours before she died, she had delivered magazines to the sick in the very hospital in which she was to bleed to death.

My mother was dead. On hearing the news, I turned my back to my companions and awkwardly walked south of camp to stare at the dead open body of Owens Lake. As I took rough southward steps, I absently wondered why it was still called a lake. Stopping, confused and raw, I felt as though there were no skin between me and the wind. That morning, the sky had turned over and called my mother's name. Now she was gone. I then looked north at the rugged wall of mountains where my friends were fasting. The stones and mountains, the clouds and sun all looked empty. The sky looked empty. I looked at my right hand; it too was empty, and it also was something that belonged to my mother. It was then I remembered these words:

> Here on this mountain I am not alone.
> For all the lives I used to be are with me.
> All the lives tell me now I have come home.

I went from her funeral to another California desert. As I entered Joshua Tree National Monument at midnight, lightning turned the landscape bone white. I went out into this second desert, intending to be alone and to fast to mark grief. As I wandered around among the rocks and crevasses for hours looking for a protected place, I realized that the protection I sought was her. The womb that had given birth to me was gone. That protection was gone, and my back was now naked. The body I had been written from was dead, and I was without authority. It was too much for me to handle so soon after her death; I returned to base camp and the fire, the hearth, another place where mother-comfort is found. There I watched her life in the fire.

That first night, I was afraid and so slept next to the fire as coyotes walked boldly through camp. After the moon set, I had the following dream: My mother is on an operating table. A friend, a surgeon in the dream, has his scalpel on her belly. I turn away in horror, but he reaches across her body to comfort me as he cuts into her. From the pool of blood in her abdomen rises a small human figure with its eyes wide and awake.

Coming out of the dream with a start, looking at the night sky and tasting the desert in my mouth, I decided to continue the journey of mourning for my mother. I also discovered I was grieving for Earth. At that moment the two, the Earth and my mother, were one body.

A short while later, I traveled to Nepal. I walked for a month in the mountains and internally carried my mother's body up and down the rugged trail. Grieving along the rivers and in the mountains, I for a time severed myself from family, friends, community, culture, and place of the familiar. I needed strange land and atmosphere in order to come to know her as an ancestor. Desert and mountains are old landscapes of space. It was in these places that her ancestral body was made, and it was to her that I offered prayer.

One evening along the trail, an old man with bright eyes and a large string of prayer beads passed through our camp. He was a *dami,* a local shaman who had come to a nearby village to heal a family. In the last light of a long, cold dusk, I asked him if I might attend the ceremony. Late that night, I and a few friends squeezed into the crowded, smoky Gurung house and watched the *dami* evoke gods of the region with drum and chant, dance their dances, handle fire, and suck out illness.

At three in the morning, I had a startling vision: My mother is wrapped up in black cobwebs; she is completely terrified and does not know what has happened or where she is. I was frozen with shock and could not move internally or externally. After a few minutes, she disappeared, and I realized with a sense of horrible regret that I had missed the opportunity of reaching through the veil that separated the living and the dead to help her. I was inconsolable.

Returning to Kathmandu, I told friends about this vision, and in compassion they arranged a Shitro ceremony in the humble Sherpa Buddhist monastery in Boudhanath. Fifteen monks and lamas with their long horns, cymbals, and offerings called my mother's "soul" back into an effigy, that she might be purified from the patterns that had caused her suffering and death. I repeatedly put my body down on the dark buttery floor as I prostrated in the gompa's shrine room, and the lamas worked their prayers and offerings in her behalf. At the end of the day, her effigy was cremated. That night I boarded a plane to California.

Two days later, in Ojai, the community gathered in the evening as a Zen priest conducted the final ceremony for my mother on the forty-ninth day of her journey through the Bardo, the intermediate state between death and rebirth. In that last night of the Bardo transit when we spoke to her across the threshold, an uncommon wind extinguished the candles on the altar, and our last words to her were punctuated with falling stars.

The journey in the Bardo of Death, according to Buddhism, is forty-nine days. During those days, I had traveled ceaselessly. My sorrow was not only for the loss of my biological mother, but also for the world. I saw the material wealth of America and its relative spiritual impoverishment. In the mountains of Nepal, I witnessed great joy in the midst of material simplicity. Meditating, fasting, living close to the Earth, walking day after day in the mountains as I worked out this sorrow, my mother's secret body was made. It was stitched together in the steps of the journey, a journey that was a rite of passage for both her and her daughter.

*   *   *

The journey doesn't end, nor do the questions. In the spring, nine months later, I fasted alone in Death Valley in eastern California asking, Which way from here? When I saw the barren landscape and walked in the rough, dusty wind to a small black cut in a wash, I thought, "This is going to be a hard one." But strangely, I felt at home and safe in this great old, dry valley. I settled into four days of deep quiet and peace. Wind, dust, sun, rain, star-filled skies, black lava rock, hearty creosote bushes, and the delicate desert five-spot were my companions. The first dawn, a small gray lizard walked up to my morning rock and sat with me. On the third morning, a lone crow flew overhead. Nine months since the death of my mother, it was time to take account.

The third evening, on seeing huge black clouds roll in from the southwest, I wrapped myself up in a tarp, feeling like a human burrito. Burrowing down into the sand, I counted the frequency of the rain drops. Any more drops per breath and I would have to move to avoid ending up as a bit of detritus at the bottom of the wash. This blue womb of plastic seemed a fitting place for my last night in the desert.

Late that night, I had an unusual dream: I am walking out to the end of an old pier to watch a school of little fish fleeing from some pursuer. Behind them comes a large creature that at first seems to be a shark. It is not a shark but a large, very old golden carp, something quite prehistoric. This great fish holds me in the gaze of its large brown left eye. He suddenly stops chasing the little fish and goes over to a piling that is holding up the pier. With his mouth, he grabs the piling and begins to shake the pier. I cannot take my eyes away from the eyes of the carp, and I begin to walk backwards rather quickly hoping to get off the pier before the whole thing collapses. Suddenly I begin to lose my eyesight, and at that moment I think, "That fish is not after the small fry; its after me!" I awaken as the pier breaks up and I sink into the water.

The past year had taught me much about yielding. I had discovered that there can only be a yield, a harvest, when one yields. The old golden fish of the depths breaks the past apart. Like the great prehistoric fish of my dream and the ocean that swallowed me, the old gold-and-black desert took me down and in. I did not resist. I reaped a harvest those four days in the desert as I accepted completely the presence of the elements. I did not have the desire to fight the sun, dust, and rain. I enjoyed the flex of the wind, the dark, rough stones, and the chill of wet nights. Fasting, I did not expend energy on grief. The losses were confirmed. Now I was just in the present, blue tarp and all. I needed to be full of care, keep my eyes open, and enjoy the reprieve from society that the wilderness provided. I had also come to complete, to give away, and to pray that my life from this day on would be lived worthily.

Sitting in this black volcanic rubble, I thanked my teachers, including the stones who had drawn sweat and prayer from me over the weeks of preparation when I purified in the Stone People Lodge (sweat lodge) for this time of solitude. The stones told me to quiet down, not move around so much, get still inside. "Endurance is a gift, not a trial. You'll be like us one day—giving yourself away as dust."

When I returned to base camp, I told my story, including the following dream, which I had on the first night back from the fast: I have entered a large hall filled with peoples from elder cultures. This is a crucial meeting about the protection of traditional ways and traditional lands. I am trying to get to my adopted father, the Lakota medicine man Grandfather Wallace Black Elk, who is sitting near the front of the room. After I enter the hall, I realize that I have to go to the toilet, and I leave the hall. When I am washing my hands, I look into the mirror and see that I have an open wound going from the corner of my right eye down my face all the way to my breastbone. I am able to look into this wound and see clearly all of the tissue structures: the blood vessels, muscles, fine ligaments, and bones. I am amazed. I had not realized that this wound was there. For a moment, I wonder who belongs to this face. Then I realize that I need to get back to the hall and see Grandfather. He is the only one who can heal this wound. On my way into the hall, I see that it is actually a doctor's office, and I know one of the young white doctors, whom I now ask to look at the wound. He communicates with his hands and in a code language to one of his partners about my condition. As this is going on, three dark heavy Indian women come to me and lay their hands on me to heal the wound. I think, "This is not enough; I must get to Grandfather." I then find myself outside the hall trying to get back in when three white nurses who have been sent by the doctor come to take me to surgery. I escape from them and make my way back into the hall and to Grandfather.

I then am awakened when Dana Fonte, my niece, and Sally Hinds, a student of Jungian psychology, come into the room. I tell the dream to Sally, and she says, "Joan, this sounds like a dream about the 'collective wound.' This is your gift and your work."

Later, when I told this dream in Council, I saw that each of us in our own way bears this World Wound. The World Wound is a collective wound that we suffer simply by being born. Buddhist practice and my study of shamanism have helped me see that we are one node in a vast web of life. As such, we are connected to each thing, and all things abide in us. Our psychological and physical afflictions are part of the stream of that beingness. On my second day in the desert, as I was walking in the late afternoon, I recalled the years of mental and physical sickness I have suffered. I asked myself then, Whose sickness is this anyway?

From one point of view, the suffering was my suffering. From another point of view, it was rooted in social, cultural, environmental, and psychological factors that were far beyond the local definition of who I am. My suffering is not unique but arises out of the ground of my culture. It arises out of the global culture and environment as well. I am part of the World's Body. If part of this body is suffering, then the world suffers.

13

Recognizing the World Wound also turns us away from a sense of exclusiveness. If we work to heal the wound in ourselves and other beings, then this part of the body of the world is also healed. Each of us carries or has carried suffering. This suffering is personal. But where is it that we end and the rest of creation begins? As part of the continuum of creation, our personal suffering is also the world's suffering. Its causes are more complex and ramified than the local self.

Suffering can also bear the fruit of compassion, the fruit of joy. I have gone into the darkness to harvest this fruit. Understanding the nature of suffering was why I practiced Buddhism, why I went into the wilds, why I worked with others. I wanted to know the roots of suffering. I also wanted to know the roots of joy, the place where we are liberated from the constraints of pain.

Going into the wound, we can see that the suffering of others is our suffering. It is not separate. We wear a common skin and have a common wound. The wound is on Earth as well as in heaven. It is in us and through us. Some of us will seek healing from those who have borne the wound more deeply than we have ourselves. That is why we go to a shaman, one who has suffered more than we have.

This wound that I bore in the dream went from the eye to the heart. It seemed to be a doorway that connected seeing and feeling. First, we have to see the wound and recognize that it is both a personal wound and a World Wound. It connects us to others and opens the eyes of compassion. Looking deeply, we can also discover that the wound is a fabrication of a history of relative causes. Suffering exists. And underneath the zones of alienation, suffering does not exist.

After the Council, four of us remained: a woman with burned hands, a woman with one breast, a woman with a long scar on her abdomen, and a woman with wounded eyes. As we looked at each other, I realized why we were there. The painter had exquisitely shaped hands; she sacrificed them to create. She said to me that my eyes were sacrificed to see. I said to the woman with one breast that the other was sacrificed that she could nourish the world. And the woman with the scarred stomach gave her guts away to know in a fearless way. Our suffering is a sacrifice, but often what we suffer from can be a gift of strength, like the shaman's wound that becomes the source of his or her compassion.

◢ ◢ ◢

The process of initiation can be likened to a "sacred catastrophe," a holy failure that actually extinguishes our alienation, our loneliness, and reveals our true nature, our love. That is why we seek initiation: to heal old wounds by reentering them in order to transform our suffering into compassion. The Dutch cultural historian Arnold van Gennep described the three phases of the journey of initiation as separation, transition, incorporation: the Severance, the Threshold, and the Return. The first phase, the Severance, is a

15

time of preparation for the ordeals and tests faced in a rite of initiation. The neophyte abandons or is severed from the familiar and begins to move into seclusion. The second phase, the Threshold, has been called "the fallow chaos." It is a time when the limits of the self are recognized and a territory is entered where the boundaries of the self are tested and broken. Incorporation means the return to society, but in a new way, with a new body and a new life.

My mother's sudden death—her abrupt severance from my life—immediately transformed the stream of routine into a river of sorrow. As she had been severed from me, I severed myself from my ordinary life. This led me to the Threshold, the second phase of a rite of passage, where I was beaten apart by grief in desert and mountain places—a grief, I discovered, that was not only for her but also for the world, for the Earth. This experience of weeds and ashes often moves one into the wilds, where the forces of the elements, as well as the presence of creatures, plants, land and water forms, the sky, and spirits conspire to break open the husk that has protected us from a deeper truth.

It is in this place of no restraint where silence and loneliness craft the soul. And then we return, purified by tears and the silence of questions that can never be answered. Poet and farmer Wendell Berry once wrote that this silence in the wilderness asks all the old answerless questions of origins and endings. It asks us who we think we are, what we think we are doing, and where we think we are going. In the silence, the world and its places and aspects are apt to become present to us. The lives of water and trees and stars surround our life "and press their obscure demands. The experience of that silence must be basic to any religious feeling. Once it is attended to, admitted into the head, one must bear a greater burden of consciousness, and knowledge—one must change one's life."

Our lives can also undergo change when we face the wall in meditation practice or when we use "teacher plants," dance, long and arduous runs, or pilgrimages to break open the husk around the psyche. At the Threshold, the gate to the unconscious, the unknown, once closed, is now open. As it opens, there appears a landscape inhabited by ancestral patterns. And in this interstice between self and other, the gods appear as forms of energy emanating from external and internal landscapes. When we are in this liminal state, we find the place where the worlds connect and flow together, where form and space, figure and ground are one.

In the Threshold we experience ourselves as a multiplex. We are both mortal and god, human and creature, wild and cultured, male and female, old and dying, and fresh and newborn. We are rough and unmade, not held together. The Threshold is where grain and chaff, beater and beaten are mixed. More explicitly, the Threshold is where we encounter death and can be renewed and restored through the unleashed primordial powers stored in the structures of the mind. These energies living in the imagination take the shapes of gods and demons, or phobias, compulsions, and madness, and become visible by our dwelling in the Threshold space between worlds. Some people think that human beings are the ground where the gods dwell, but I am sure that it is not in us but in the interworld between us and sacred space that the gods finally arise.

The third phase of a rite of passage is the Return. But the Return is to a place we never left, although we did not know that we were there all along. In the womb, a physical umbilical cord attaches us to our mother. After we are born, we sustain a wound when this cord is cut and we are separated from the maternal organism. We also have a social umbilicus, which ties us to society. This cord is cut in the process of the wounding of initiation. But there is another umbilicus that cannot be cut. This cord, like a great lattice, ties us to each thing that dwells through us and in which we dwell. It is a life cord or net that connects us to the womb of creation. We live in and through the body of this latticelike cord just as we live in the Milky Way that stretches across the sky. This is what we return to, this life thread that sews together the fabric of our world. Here we can stitch together the robe of society with the stuff of creation to restore and renew the life of our peoples and help them see that culture only blossoms in the field of nature. Our lives awaken in the body of this invisible, pervasive, and subtle cord.

So I say, "Seek initiation." When we enter the self by penetrating with our awareness the deeper zones of mind and body, we see that the wound that has opened in our psyches and on the body of Earth is a continuum of suffering. Self and relationships, self and setting are not separate. They are a "unity in process."

As the environmental aspects of our alienation from the ground of life become increasingly apparent, the social, physical, mental, and spiritual correlates rise into view. We all suffer in one way or another. Consciously or unconsciously, we wish to be liberated from this suffering. Some of us will attempt to transcend suffering. Some of us will be overwhelmed and imprisoned by it. Some of us in our attempts to rid ourselves of suffering will create more pain. In the way of shamans and Buddhists, we are encouraged to face fully whatever form our suffering takes, to confirm it, and, finally, to let it ignite our compassion and wisdom. We ask, How can we work with this suffering, this "World Wound"? How can our experience of this wound connect us to the web of creation? And how can this wound be a door to compassion and compassionate action?

Rites of initiation are those great zones of darkness that make the unclear, the contradictory, the polluted, and the changeable the ground of renewal. They are the occasions of fruitful darkness. Marie-Louise von Franz says, "The first step is generally falling into the dark place, and usually appears in a dubious or negative form,—falling into something, or being possessed by something. . . . The Shamans say that being a medicine man begins by falling into the power of the demons; the one who pulls out of the dark place becomes the medicine man, and the one who stays in it is the sick person. . . . You can take every psychological illness as an initiation. Even the worst things you fall into are an effort of initiation, for you are in something which belongs to you."

Blessed are the men and women
who are planted on your earth, in your
 garden
who grow as your trees and flowers grow,
who transform their darkness to light.
Their roots plunge into darkness;
their faces turn toward the light.

Song of Solomon, translated
by Stephen Mitchell

2

The Way of Silence

I have a feeling that my boat
has struck, down there in the depths,
against a great thing.
    And nothing
happens! Nothing . . . Silence . . . Waves . . .

 —Nothing happens? Or has everything happened,
and are we standing now, quietly, in the new life?
  Juan Ramón Jiménez, translated by Robert Bly

Crossing the Sahara in my late twenties on my way to the Dogon, I came to know what it was to live in a world with an endless horizon, a place of no boundaries, where silence roared in the ears. Each mile across the great desert took me more surely into the unknown. To the north of me, far to the north, was Algeria's Oran. Far to the south was the Niger River. But between Oran and the river was a vast territory where the gods dwelled, the gods of sun, sky, sand, and space, gods of rolling, orange, looming dunes and gods of nights punctuated with the crescent moon.

In the turning of this sea of sand by day and in the turning of the stars in the night sky, in the perfectly clear silences that stood like sentinels guarding sleep, I watched the world I knew leave me and another world appear, a world beyond my control. I moved across a frontier, a secret territory of the unfamiliar that humans see only through supernatural eyes. It was an unpredictable world, a home for chaos, a place of ashes and old sand stirred by strong and fickle winds. An initiation, this journey across the Sahara cut me away from my world and drew me into the body of indeterminacy. It also drew me into immaculate silence.

The poet Kathleen Raine once suggested, "It is not that birds speak, but men learn silence." I think that it is when we learn silence that the birds speak to us. Fertile silence is like a placenta nourishing us from both emptiness and its connectedness with the greater organism of creation. Indeed, one aspect of silence is emptiness, and yes, it is often lonely. In the presence of silence, the conditioned self rattles and scratches. It begins to crumble like old leaves or worn rock. If we have courage, we take silence as medicine to cure us from our social ills, the suffering of self-centered alienation. In silence, sacred silence, we stand naked like trees in winter, all our secrets visible under our skin. And like winter's tree, we appear dead but are yet alive.

In silence and solitude, in the emptiness of hunger and the worthiness of the wilds, men and women have taken refuge in the continuum of bare truth. John Muir once wrote, "I only went out for a walk, and finally concluded to stay out till sundown, for going out, I found, was really going in." Silence is where we learn to listen, where we learn to see. Holding silence, being held by stillness, Buddhists and tribal people go alone to the wilderness "to stop and see," to renew their vision, to enter the mind ground, to hear the truth, to return to the knowledge of the extensiveness of self and the truth of no self. The ceremony of the vision fast and the eremitic and yogic traditions of Buddhism are not solipsistic endeavors. Often we must go outside society to confirm that we live inside the continuum of creation. One seeks solitude to know relatedness. There the unknown, the unarticulated, the unpredictable, the uncontrollable appear as protectors of truth, protectors of the present.

The Lakota John Fire Lame Deer felt that silence was the ground of his medicine:

> The wicasa wakan loves the silence, wrapping it around himself like a blanket—a loud silence with a voice like thunder which tells him of many things. Such a man likes to be in a place where there is no sound but the humming of insects. He sits facing the West, asking for help. He talks to the plants and they answer him. He listens to the voices of the Wama Kaskan—all those who move upon the earth, the animals. He is at one with them. From all living beings something flows into him all the time, and something flows from him. I don't know where or what, but it's there. I know.

The Huichol shaman's experience of solitude and silence is rooted in the space that one

25

encounters as the gap between worlds. This territory is symbolized as a blooming flower, an image of the *nearika,* the "visionary doorway," that separates ordinary and visionary consciousness. Although I have never seen a staircase or a rose in the land of the Huichols, the event of ecstatic ascent and the sacred flower of vision are two elements arising in the course of shamanic solitude:

> climbed the blue staircase up to the sky
> climbed where the roses were opening
> > where roses were speaking
>
> heard nothing nothing to hear
> > heard silence
>
> i climbed where the roses were singing
> > where the gods were waiting
> > blue staircase up in the sky
>
> but heard nothing nothing to hear
> > heard silence silence

When we sever ourselves from society in a rite of change, there is an invisible door that we pass through that has no words on the other side. On this side of the door, says García Lorca, "Our eyes remain on the surface, like water flowers, behind which we hide / our trembling bodies floating in an unseen world." It is this door to the depths that opens when we die. When we pass through this door, we always lose something. Something must be sacrificed. If it is the door between life and death, we sacrifice our physical body, and if it is the door of initiation, we sacrifice our social body. This door also separates and joins the living and the dead. Creation requests that we open this door.

I believe it is through stillness and silence that the door opens. Inside the secret room, we weave the threads of understanding into the cloth of culture. However, in our world neither silence nor solitude are held to be of much value. "All is seared with trade; bleared, smeared with toil; / And wears man's smudge and shares man's smell," wrote Gerard Manley Hopkins. Yet silence and solitude are the very basis for our engagement with the world. They are expressed in the experiences of inquiry and listening, nonviolence and nonduality, patience and concentration, connectedness and intimacy, authenticity and stillness, understanding and compassion, and seeing beyond language and intuition.

If immaculate silence is a placenta that nourishes us, then solitude is a secret womb that wraps around us and holds us in our place. A psychic landscape of emptiness, it is a place where we are gestated, and from which we are born into the greater womb of creation. Alone in the wilderness, the fire of the sun can burn us; the rains can freeze us; the winds can blow our sense away; Earth can fill us with fear. We are initiated and purified by the elements, empty-handed and undefended. Fasting, our bellies hungry, we feel closer to the bone of life and under the skin of death. The poisons of our body and mind rise up from the depths. They are the stale bitter taste on the root of our tongue. This stuff of a past not worthily lived is also medicine.

Without food, we seek nourishment in the present and in the silence; the sandy wash, the varnished stone, the dark hard lava, the small gray cloud, all are food for us. We also begin to derive nourishment from our ancestral past. In a Ute song, it is said, "In our bones is the rock itself; in our blood is the river; our skin contains the shadow of every living thing we ever came across. This is what we brought with us long ago." We are the sum of our ancestors. Our roots stretch back to blue-green algae; they stretch to the stars. They ultimately reach the void. Between the great original emptiness, the ancestral void, and the body that reads these words, there stand number-less generations of inorganic and organic forms. As geological history is written on a canyon wall, this history is inscribed in our psyches. Silence and solitude enjoin us to remember our whole and great body.

To know this, the mountain and desert, forest and frozen lands are where shamans have sought vision and meditators and monks have sought to realize their genuine mind ground. The Eskimo shaman Igjugarjuk said, "When I was to be an anatkoq, I chose suffering through the two things that are most dangerous to us humans, suffering through hunger and suffering through cold. . . . True wisdom is only to be found far away from people, out in the great solitude, and it is not found in play but only through suffering. Solitude and suffering open the human mind, and there-fore a shaman seeks his wisdom there."

Don José told me years ago, "I have pursued my apprenticeship for sixty-four years. During these years, many, many times have I gone to the mountains alone. Yes, I have endured great suffering during my life. Yet to learn to see, to learn to hear, you must do this—go into the wilderness alone. For it is not I who can teach the ways of the gods. Such things are learned only in solitude."

In the Essene Gospel of John, Jesus said:

Fast and pray fervently, seeking the power of the living God for your healing. While you fast, eschew the Sons of Men and seek our Earthly Mother's angels, for he that seeks shall find. Seek the fresh air of the forest and of the fields, and there in the midst of them shall you find the angels of the air. Put off your shoes and your clothing and suffer the angel of air to embrace all your body. Then breathe long and deeply, that the angel of air . . . shall cast out of your body all uncleanesses which defiled it without and within.

Returning from the wilds, we can learn the craft of ceremony from a teacher and make attempts to conceptualize the knowledge of nonduality learned in the wilderness. But the true muscle of learning strengthens when we are alone, when we face our trials truly alone and find comfort and courage in solitude. Steven Foster once said to me that loneliness is the teacher of giving. Aloneness teaches us how we are really connected to and interdepending with everything. Paradoxical though it may seem, solitude reveals our interrelatedness. Buddhist and shaman alike share this path of paradox.

For some, silence is a medicine. For others, silence seems like a poison and is actually feared. We in the "developed" world seem to have many auditory strategies that insulate us from the presence of silence, simplicity, and solitude. When I return to Western culture after time in desert, mountain, or forest, I discover how we have filled our world with a multiplicity of noises, a symphony of forgetfulness that keeps our own thoughts and realizations, feelings and intuitions out of audible range. Perhaps we fear that with silence we might hear the cries of our own suffering and the suffering in the world. The sound of suffering is covered over by the ceaseless song of longing for more; the mindless tunes of elevator music; the crackling of "news"; the grind of transiting vehicles; endless chatter in hallways, in coffee shops, in our minds; the remorseless electrical hum and whir tuning us to the shared frequency of the developed world.

Indeed, we seem to have an aversion not only to silence but also to space, to emptiness of both space and time. Time in our culture is scheduled to the minute lest we "have time on our hands." The television set, the electronic hearth, holds young and old in a time trance. We even try to fit birth and death into a schedule. We fill our homes and offices with "things" and "more things," and the overflow finds its way into crowded storage lockers, where it is forgotten.

An individual who chooses simplicity, silence,

or solitude is frequently assumed to be depressed, angry, or in some way impoverished. We are afraid of our loneliness, this solitude that might make us feel empty. But empty of what? we must ask ourselves.

I have noticed that the more "developed" the world, the noisier it gets. I remember one morning after a ceremony in the Huichol village of El Colorín when I paid my neighbor in the next hut to turn off his battery-operated record player. For days and nights we had chanted and danced in celebration of the first corn. In this ceremony, one's whole body is restructured through mind-transforming plants and chants to welcome into the village the new maize, the staff of life. We ourselves became like the corn—vulnerable, fresh and new, food for the world. At the end of all this, I did not have the heart or guts to offer myself to the structuring of the so-called developed world through its music. I needed to be "medicined" by the old ways before I made the return journey to my culture of origin. I also needed some silence to absorb the rich dye in which I had been washed during those past few days.

Lying in my hut, I realized that there was a kind of war of the worlds going on in this small Huichol village. The shamans represented the mind of the visionary realm, a mind of no boundaries, a big mind of silence. The Mexican-trained Huichol school teachers represented the rational mind of development and progress. We Anglos who had made it to this remote settlement presented an odd if not threatening spectacle to the "educated" teachers who were trying to wean their people from "superstition."

By this time in the mid-seventies, I had realized that I had no choice but to enter the world of tribal peoples as friend and student rather than researcher and scholar. I had something to learn from sacred plants, from ceremony, from solitude and stillness, and from the silence of space. I had to yield to something in myself that would not appear while I was in Western culture. I yearned to be with old people who, like my grandmother, could capture me with their stories. Like so many of my friends, not only was I alienated from what was around me, but I was also unconscious of the secret body within me. It was through the teachings of the Huichol *mara'akáme* Don José and the Dogon elder Ogobara, through traveling far away from my local home, my local culture, and taking refuge in silence and solitude of desert, mountain, and forest, that I discovered all creation was my kin.

In my solitude
I have seen things very clearly
that were not true.

Antonio Machado,
translated by Robert Bly

3

The Way of Traditions

These things are one.
They are a unity.
They are ourselves.

Ramón Medina Silva

In the mid-seventies, I traveled across the deserts of northern Mexico to the Mountains of the Western Mothers, the Sierra Madre Occidental, where Huichol Indians live. The rainy season was just over, making the narrow trail up into the mountains not impossible for a donkey but nearly so for the horse I had been given to ride. When fifteen Huichols met me and two friends at the foot of the mountain to escort us to their village, I was honored with the horse, a white one with western saddle.

For several years prior to this visit, I had raised money to buy beans for the villagers of El Colorín, the home of Don José Ríos. The delicate bean plant could not survive the herbicide supplied by the Mexican government to clear jungle growth for planting corn, and the people of this area were suffering from malnutrition. My fundraising for them had provided beans as well as a cow, chickens, donkeys, riding tack, and a fine white horse.

It seemed as if I was to be something of a special guest in the village, and for a moment I felt like the bride of the Mesoamerican god-king Quetzalcoatl. But this archetype soon turned sour as this "fine white horse" proved less than worthy for the trail. My sense of humility was further deepened by the horse's height, which set me at a level to be caught in wet branches and the large, sticky spider webs woven between them. It wasn't long before I realized I was in for the usual reality test that tribal cultures put one through.

Late that night I arrived at Don José's small village of El Colorín, near the top of an unnamed mountain. The old man, whose grown children had visited me in California over the years, was doing a healing for one of his relatives when we arrived. Don José and his wife, Josefa, invited me to stay the night in their small hut, but I insisted on sleeping on the dirt patio in front of their dwelling. Not long into an exhausted sleep, I found myself surrounded by pigs and dogs who were aggressively curious. These folks don't sleep on their patios in their village. I now knew why.

I had gone to El Colorín to meet Don José, an old mountain corn farmer and doctor. It was the season of the harvest of the first maize and squash and the Ceremony of the Drum, or as the Huichols call it Tatéi Néiya, "Our Mother Ceremony." In the course of this annual rite, children, symbolized by the first corn and squash, are sung to the Home of the Mother Goddesses and into Wirikúta, the

Huichol's original homeland, where the peyote cactus grows, and the land of Our Elder Brother Deer. This magical flight of the children is the story of the great pilgrimage to Huichol paradise. It is also an occasion for children to be cured. Curing in the world of the Huichols focuses on the prevention of ills that result from forgetting the ancient ways or violating taboos. Huichols feel that their traditions maintain balance and harmony in the world. Their myths, which give shape to Huichol ceremonial life, are a reminder that the well-being of the people depends on the proper regard for their customs, a theme important to this book.

According to Huichol mythology, in ancient times after the world had been put in order by Our Grandfather Fire, Grandmother Growth, and the Divine Deer Person Kauyumari, Our Grandfather Fire called the gods into council. All of the gods were suffering from various illnesses, and they assembled so that Grandfather Fire, the first shaman, could cure them. In Council, Grandfather divined that the gods had not followed the traditions, had not made the pilgrimage to the Sacred Land of Peyote. Only by doing so would they "find their life." So the gods prepared themselves for this difficult journey by fasting, abstaining from sex and salt, taking ritual ablutions, and making votive arrows and gourds. The gods prepared themselves for the pilgrimage as Huichols still prepare themselves today.

The gods then left the comfort of their village and went on the sacred journey. After many days of traveling and near death, the Ancient Ones arrived at the edge of a spring-fed lake. From a nearby rancho, Huichol women emerged bearing gourds of sacred water and tortillas. These were Our Mothers, owners of rain and all terrestrial waters.

After drinking the sacred water and washing their heads, after being nourished by the holy corn, the gods, being of one heart, traveled into Wirikúta. The Great Shaman, Tatewarí, saw Elder Brother Deer on the first altar far in the distance, and though Our Elder Brother transformed himself and tried to escape to the second altar, he was not able to do so. Setting up their snares, the Old Ones ran him down, and they saw that where he left his footprints peyote grew.

As Our Elder Brother Deer lay dying, they caught the radiant energy streaming from his head and were strengthened by it. In fact, Elder Brother Deer did not die, but was peyote. They ground his antlers and drank of this, and this was also peyote. His hooves were peyote, his flesh and bones, all were peyote.

After singing and dancing and seeing many beautiful things in the desert, they climbed the sacred mountain and made an offering to the place where Our Father Sun was born. Wearing the skin of the holy deer, they returned to their village by way of many holy places. They brought with them the sacred water from the springs of Our Mothers and the wonderful gift of peyote. In that way they returned to where they started, but now they were fully healed, as Tatewarí had told them.

Huichols feel that humans, like the gods, can

fall ill if they do not make the annual journey to their sacred homeland. Such a journey purifies and makes new the people and the gods. It renews the land as well, in the sense that its sacredness is remembered and celebrated. The ancient customs of the Huichols, and most particularly the Drum Ceremony, readies children for what it is "to be Huichol," what it means to live a life of beauty and harmony. It reveals the single thread of the past and the present. It makes the imaginary and mythic real and infuses life with intense meaning. As Ramón Medina Silva said, "Our symbols, the deer, the peyote, the maize of five colors—all, all that you have seen, there in Wirikúta, when we go to hunt the peyote—these are beautiful. They are beautiful because they are right." These Ancient Ones—deer, corn, peyote—still feed the body and soul of Huichol people. They are at the center of Huichol culture, a holy trinity that actually sustains the people and their way of life. The Huichols say that is why these three are beautiful.

The myth of the journey to Wirikúta is at once a sacred history and a collective dream. The history recounts how the Ancient Ones, the gods of the Huichols, fell ill through forgetting yet, returning to the traditional ways, were healed. The myth is also a collective dream reminding the people of the value of the continuity of traditions, particularly as they apply to place, to sacred and real locales.

As a story that is a display of the human psyche, this myth may be of some interest to non-Huichols as well. First, it is told on a ceremonial occasion associated with the healing of children and the harvesting of the firstfruits of corn and squash, which, like the children, are healed of the ill effects of the masculine Sun, among other things. Our Father Sun, according to the Huichols, needs to be at a correct distance from the Earth; otherwise, its arrows will cause great illness to befall the fruits of the Earth, including human beings. Ceremony is a way to keep things in order and to honor the powers that bring about harmony.

The story is about the gods who have lost touch with the past and how the traditions of their Ancestors confirm the sacredness of life. They have abandoned, as we have, the holy pilgrimage to Paradise, a journey that requires immense sacrifice. They have forgotten to offer thanks to the Old Ones, who are encoded into the landscape that one passes through on the way to Wirikúta. Most of all, they have forgotten the Mystery of the Mothers of Waters, Flowers, and Children, the gift of feminine corn and water that is offered at the threshold of the Other World.

We are like those gods, ill and disgruntled, alienated from the view that all of life is sacred. We are sitting around in our workplaces, in doctors' offices, in our churches and temples feeling out of sorts. Indeed, many of us are desperately sick. We complain about the state of the world and are fearful of the state of our bodies, our families, the economy, and the Earth. Over the years, we have become lazy, complacent, and depressed and, like the gods, have forgotten to tend the hearth of the Fire of our awareness and to enter the Waters of the Feminine.

In the myth, the gods prevail upon Grandfather Fire, co-creator of this world, to help them.
Grandfather knows what to do. The dangerous
and arduous pilgrimage to the original homeland
must be made. But it needs to be done correctly.
We, like the gods of the Huichols who forgot their
roots, are being asked to give up what we have
gotten used to. We cannot take these worldly elements to Paradise. It is enough just to get there;
carrying our possessions with us would be too
much. And so they go, the gods—lighter for fasting, abstaining from sex, taking ritual baths, con-
fessing their wrongdoings. The gods go, led by
Kauyumari, the deer-trickster and ally of the
shaman, and Tatewarí, Grandfather Fire.

We go to Paradise with the help of trickster
and reconciler and the Fire of our awareness, Our
Grandfather. Cleaner, lighter, because we have
sacrificed, we are able to see the holy places of the
Ancient Ones along the way. We offer respect and
give gifts to that which marks continuity in the
web of creation, to the sacred places where the
gods dwell, where our ancestors have worshiped.
We remember and are restored through acts of remembering. And we are exhausted, near death, so
difficult is the journey. But at our most desperate
moment, we arrive at the place of the Sacred
Waters.

There we find a familiar dwelling, a home of
comfort, and from here the Sacred Mothers of the
Waters emerge with female offerings of water to
slake thirst and the staff of life, corn, to drive
away hunger. Wine and bread, the body of our
Savior. In the case of the Huichols, the body of

Our Savioresses, the holy waters of our mothers and the sacred feminine corn. This is what is given when we have sacrificed and purified and journeyed to the place of the feminine. Receiving these gifts of physical and spiritual sustenance, simple though they may seem, we can enter the holy land and be given the vision of communion that is bestowed there.

When we enter Paradise, yet another sacrifice is required. This time, what will be offered is Our Elder Brother Deer, he who has helped set the world in order. It is Grandfather Fire who sees and slays the Magical Deer. And in so doing, Deer is transformed into peyote. Equated with the feminine corn and the masculine deer, peyote is the principle of male and female combined that when eaten evokes the vision of unity that the Huichols say is "their life." The journey to Wirikúta, the sacred land of peyote, is "to find their life."

To "find our life," according to one interpretation of the myth, we must stop sitting around and complaining. We are called to prepare ourselves through sacrifice to journey to the feminine at the gates of Paradise, be cleansed and strengthened in heart by the gifts from the maternal. In this way, we can be reborn into heaven on Earth. Here we learn that death is a transformation of matter into spirit when we sacrifice that which seems most precious to us, the masculine deer who helped put the world together. Through Our Elder Brother's sacrifice and his subsequent transformation, we enter the vision of the sacred marriage of Heaven and Earth, a world of balance and harmony. We then don the skin of the deer—take on the identity of the one who has set the world in order, the one who is both trickster and reconciler—and return to our homes to enter the circle of life and creation.

▲ ▲ ▲

My days in the Huichol Sierra are a wild and bittersweet memory—the emaciated dogs ("They make better hunters if you don't feed 'em"), the heavy rains driving all the dogs (and their fleas) under the eaves of my hut (no local would put up with that kind of familiarity), the social gaffe I made by bathing nude in a spring just outside the village (I found myself the laughingstock of the village before I was even dry), and endless perfect meals of tortillas and beans.

The mountaintops all around were punctuated with lightning. The vivid embroidery of costumes came alive as men and women danced around Tatewarí, Our Grandfather Fire. The altar with offerings of tamales to the gods and the life-journey thread joining these offerings to the gods' eyes were both a protection and a doorway to a world of visions. This thread was twined with white tufts of cotton, the souls of the children being sung to the godland. They also represent the clouds of the Rain Goddess, who will help to bring the corn and the harvest.

The old man Matsuwa (Pulse) was missing right hand and forearm. His left hand was twisted and withered from a machete accident. His friends and relatives insisted that he was one day older than God. No matter his age, over the years that I knew him, his hair became darker and darker and his wit sharper and sharper. He was an amazing and naughty old man, full of love and jokes. He had energy to spare and was always ready for the next adventure.

So my days were spent, as they are in parts like these, doing the ordinary: sitting around and listening to gossip as women and men beaded, embroidered, or wove; visiting the cornfields, the *milpa,* and admiring the big wet ears of maize ready for harvest; slicing squash and melon and trying to learn how to make tortillas (failing the lesson); sweeping hoards of small roaches out of Mariana's chimneyless kitchen; and helping here and there with the preparation for the Drum Ceremony. I was also dealing with an incredible infestation of fleas. These creatures didn't seem to like Huichols, but I was certainly to their taste. Thus time passed with the simple, the poetic, the absurd and frustrating weaving together in different combinations.

Then one day, the tempo shifted. The Drum Ceremony was under way. The ceremony took place in the hamlet above the old man's patio. He sat on his shaman's chair hour after hour in this three-day ceremony, just simply held his place like a mountain. To his right and left was a group of elders who laughed and sang and consulted each other throughout. Among them was the spectacular sorcerer Natcho Pistola, a strikingly handsome man, respected and feared by the villagers. Years later, I learned from Don José that he had given me away that night to the old sorcerer. (Fortunately, I remained ignorant of this arrangement until long after Natcho had passed into the other world.) This gathering of shamans and sorcerers created a world of bright and dark shapes as they recalled in chant the origin story of peyote, the sacred center and focus of Huichol culture.

During the ceremony, the shaman sings the children to Paradise. And in doing this, he lays the map of this sacred and very real geography into the nervous system of all those who are there to listen. He sings,

Look, you *tevainuríxi* [sacred children]
Surely we are going to where the *peyoteros*
    have gone
On the pilgrimage of the peyote.
Who knows if we are going to arrive or not,
Because the journey there is dangerous.

One must fly in order to walk over the wind
Light as the air,
To fly as birds.
We will make camp
There under the highest trees
That you see there
And one sees them. . . .
One hears the whirring of their wings.

45

The chant continued hour after hour, taking us through the steps of the pilgrimage, to each power place, and then to Wirikúta where Elder Brother is sacrificed and peyote is eaten. The shaman Ramón Medina Silva explained to Barbara Myerhoff that although the *mara'akáme* is describing in chant the sacred geography of the journey, it is Maxa Kwaxí–Kauyumari (Elder Brother Deer Tail) who is magically relating to the shaman what he sees as he helps the shaman and the souls of the children on their way.

At one point, I made a move to leave the ceremonial ground. I felt quite ill and wanted to make my way to the brush to get sick. Awkwardly, I began to push myself up from the ground where I was sitting, when Don José barked at me, "Don't move! You will break the net of power. . . . Juana, put your mind into the Fire."

I did. And what I saw was a world that was alive with shining filaments emanating from and connecting everything. This beautiful world was flowing with brilliant threads of light, and for one moment I thought it was my own nervous system that had somehow extended beyond the boundary of my body. Then I was sure it was the nervous system of the planet.

Ramón Medina Silva had once said of the ceremonial experience with peyote, "These things are one. They are a unity. They are ourselves." At that moment, I not only knew what he meant, I was what he meant. The "net of power" was really a net of communion, which had caught creation in it. I then looked up at Don José and saw into him, and I saw him seeing me see him. It was like finding oneself in a hall of mirrors where one is caught in a resonance of infinite reflections. Through his eyes, which were like bright flowers, I seemed to see all that had passed in ancient times. I also saw myself. I was like a piece of old turquoise that had been passed from hand to hand over the generations. My body was bright blue space, and ultimately I belonged only to Earth.

The last night of the ceremony in El Colorín, we danced around the fire where the green maize and squash were cooking. We thanked the Mother Rains and danced until dawn. In the morning, the squash and corn were ceremonially cleansed by the old shaman, and then all of us, children and adults, circled the fire and were ritually purified by wild flowers and precious spring water, as was the corn and squash. In this way, we were made new again.

Several years after the ceremony, while visiting California, Don José reminded me of this ceremony in his village of El Colorín. He gazed at me for a short time and said, "Juana, you have seen the flower of vision on my face. . . . In that flower is a mountain from which the Sun was born. You should always look for that mountain. It will purify you, this great one."

I recalled that moment during the Drum Ceremony when I looked up into the old man's face and saw an unending flower of numberless generations of healers carrying the old Ways through time and space. This flower was both his mind and a gateway to a kind of humorous impartiality free of any tradition. When I asked him about the mountain, he laughed and said that one day I would be sacrificed on such a mountain and then would return as the sun. Little did I realize then that I would over the next decade go to mountain after mountain seeking my life.

We are all,
We are all the children of
a brilliant colored flower,
a flaming flower.
And there is no one,
There is no one,
Who regrets who we are.

Huichol song

4

The Way of the Mountain

My words are tied in one
with the great mountains
    Yokuts prayer, collected by A. L. Kroeber

Everybody has a geography that can be used for change. That is why we travel to far-off places. Whether we know it or not, we need to renew ourselves in territories that are fresh and wild. We need to come home through the body of alien lands. For some, these journeys of change are taken intentionally and mindfully. They are pilgrimages, occasions when Earth heals us directly.

Pilgrimage has been for me, and many others, a form of inquiry in action. Although there is usually a particular destination to go to when on pilgrimage, it is the journey itself that is the thing. Once in dokusan (Zen interview) with Richard Baker Roshi, I asked the following question: "'Going to the temple, you take the path. Entering the temple you leave the path.' What does this mean?" Without a pause, his response was "Joan, the path is the temple."

People have traveled over this Earth with a heart of inquiry for millennia. They have sung through the land as a living being, offered themselves, their steps, their voices and prayers as acts of purification that opened them to an experience of connectedness. Whether it is Huichol peoples of Mexico who annually journey to Wirikúta, or Australian aborigines, whose song-lines connect dreamings across thousands of miles, or Hindu pilgrims who make their way to the Mother Ganges or Shiva's Abode, or Buddhist pilgrims who reconstitute the life of the Buddha by visiting the groves and mountains, towns and villages where his birth, realizations, teachings, and passing occurred, pilgrimage is a remembering in the passing through of sacred time and sacred space.

Mountains have long been a geography for pilgrimage, places where peoples have been humbled and strengthened. They are symbols of the Sacred Center. Many have traveled to them in order to find the concentrated energy of Earth and to realize the strength of unimpeded space. Viewing a mountain at a distance or walking around its body, we can see its shape, know its profile, survey its surrounds. The closer you come to the mountain, the more it disappears. The mountain begins to lose its shape as you near it. Its body begins to spread out over the landscape, losing itself to itself. On climbing the mountain, the mountain continues to vanish. It vanishes in the detail of each step. Its crown is buried in space. Its body is buried in the breath.

On reaching the mountain's summit, we can

ask, What has been attained? The top of the mountain? Big view? But the mountain has already disappeared. Going down the mountain, we can ask, What has been attained? Going down the mountain? The closer we are to the mountain, the more the mountain disappears. The closer we are to the mountain, the more the mountain is realized.

Mountain's realization comes through the details of the breath. Mountain appears in each step. Mountain then lives inside our bones, inside our heartdrum. It stands like a huge mother in the atmosphere of our minds. Mountain draws ancestors together in the form of clouds. Heaven, Earth, and Human meet in the raining of the past. Heaven, Earth, and Human meet in the winds of the future. Mountain Mother is a birth gate that joins the above and below. She is a prayer house. She is a mountain. Mountain is a mountain.

Mountains are extolled not only for their qualities but also for their effect on those who relate to them. Taking refuge in them, pilgrimaging to them, and walking around or ascending them has long been a way for the shaman and the Buddhist to purify and realize the mind of the mountain. The surface of inner and outer landscape, of the above and below, meet in the mountain body. The sense of place is confirmed in the mountain body. The spirit of place is confirmed when the mountain disappears into the landscape of the mind. Thus one reveres mountains.

Some of us are drawn to mountains the way the moon draws the tide. Both the great forests and the mountains live in my bones. They have taught me, humbled me, purified me, and changed me: Mount Fuji, Mount Shasta, Mount Kailas, the Schreckhorn, Kanchenjunga. Mountains are abodes for ancestor and deity. They are places where energy is discovered, made, acquired, and spent. Mountains are symbols, as well, of enduring truth and of the human quest for spirit. I was told long ago to spend time with mountains.

The Sung dynasty painter-poet Kuo-hsi (c. 1060–1075) once wrote of mountains,

Inexhaustible is their mystery.
In order to grasp their creations
One must love them utterly,
Study their essential spirit diligently,
And never cease contemplating them
And wandering among them.

So-o is reputed to have said, "The mountain it-self is a mandala. Practice self-reflection intently amid the undefiled stones, trees, streams, and veg-etation, losing yourself in the great body of the Supreme Buddha." Mountains are felt to be the least tamed of all terrains, environments of un-mediated potency. They are places where beings of every description complete themselves. This activ-ity of fulfillment can be manifested in wise wild-ness, as in the wanderings of the high-altitude monk-poet Han-shan, whose clear view of nondu-ality was exemplified by the enduring strength, fine atmosphere, and freedom of mountains:

I climb the road to Cold Mountain,
The road to Cold Mountain that never ends.
The valleys are long and strewn with stones;
The streams broad and banked with thick
    grass.
Moss is slippery, though no rain has fallen;
Pines sigh, but it isn't the wind.
Who can break from the snare of the world
And sit with me among the white clouds?

As a student of Buddhism and a mountain wanderer, I have been deeply affected by the writings of Zen Master Dogen (1200–1253), the ancestor and founder of the Soto School of Japan. Dogen Zenji wrote a remarkable vernacular text, the *Shobogenzo (The Treasury of the True Dharma Eye),* which includes the "Mountains and Rivers Sutra." Reading it, I learned something about mountains and something about mind.

Dogen says that mountains and rivers at this very moment are a revelation of Truth. Mountains are conditioned, relative, and connecting Beings and are perfect exactly as they are. Mountains and rivers, in their relative and absolute nature, have no identity that is separate or distinct from anything else. Mountains express rivers, and rivers express mountains. Mountains are hidden in rivers, and rivers are hidden in mountains. Mountains and rivers are mandalas that have all qualities as potentials within them.

Dogen realized that the activity of mountains and rivers, like Buddhist spiritual life, was not in

the world but of the world itself. From this perspective, mountains and rivers are not only
Buddha's true nature but share in the great body
of all true nature.

Several months before he wrote the "Moun-
tains and Rivers Sutra," Dogen composed the
*Keisei sanshoku (Sound of the Valley, Form of the
Mountain),* a work based on this verse by the poet
Su Tung-p'o:

> The sound of the valley stream is his long,
>   broad tongue,
> The mountain, his Pure Body.
> This evening's eighty-four thousand verses—
> How will I tell them tomorrow?

Dogen tells us,

> Mountains and rivers at this very moment are
> the actualization of the word of the ancient
> Buddhas. Each, abiding in its phenomenal
> expression, realizes completeness. Because
> mountains and rivers have been active since
> before the Empty Aeon, they are alive in this
> present moment. Because they have been the
> self since before form arose they are the real-
> ization of freedom. . . . We must carefully
> investigate the walking of the blue mountains,
> the walking of the self.

And he goes on,

> Thus, the accumulated virtues [of the moun-
> tain] represent its name and form, its very

lifeblood. There is a mountain walk and a mountain flow, and there is a time when the mountain gives birth to a mountain child. The mountains become the Buddhas and Ancestors, and it is for this reason that the Buddhas and Ancestors have thus appeared.

Dogen ends the Sutra with the advice that

there are mountains hidden in jewels; there are mountains hidden in marshes, mountains hidden in the sky; there are mountains hidden in mountains. There are mountains hidden in hiddenness. An ancient Buddha has said, "Mountains are mountains and rivers are rivers." The meaning of these words is not that mountains are mountains but that mountains are mountains. Investigate mountains thoroughly. When you investigate mountains thoroughly, this is the work of the mountains. Such mountains and rivers of themselves become wise persons and sages.

In Dogen's world of mountains and rivers, of plum blossoms and bright moons, everything is the body of the Buddha, everything has the sound of Truth in it. Hidden within each thing is every other thing, like Indra's Net of Jewels. Dogen sought to convey all the basic activity of the world as mutual and enlightened. The mountains are the Buddhas and Ancestors writes Dogen: "The blue mountains devote themselves to the investigation of walking; the East Mountain devotes itself to the study of 'moving over the water.' Hence, this study is the mountain's own study. The mountains, unchanged in body and mind, maintaining their own mountain countenance, have always been traveling about studying themselves."

Before Dogen and after Dogen, in Tibet, China, and Japan, wilderness, and most particularly the greatness of mountains, has called rustic ascetics to their strength and stillness. The Chinese ideograph for *hsien* and Japanese *sen* is made up of two parts, one meaning person, the other meaning mountain. In Taoism and in Ch'an Buddhism, the *hsien* was a spiritual practitioner who used the mountain as a birth gate to awakening. Japan, like China, had a number of spiritual schools inspired by mountain mind. The tradition of Taoist naturalism and Esoteric Buddhist cosmology and rituals combined in the background of Shinto asceticism to give rise to Shugendo. The ascetic practitioners of the Shugendo sect are called *yamabushi* or "those who lie down in the mountains."

In the Esoteric Buddhist schools of Tendai and Shingon, with which Shugendo sects were affiliated, ceremony and extreme, intensive practices are a means for the mountain to be realized. These mountain bodies are worshiped through the activities of pilgrimage, fasting, running, prayer, and solitude, yet it is the mountains themselves that do the true teaching. Here the teachings are directly incorporated, completely embodied. Although the modern world has turned some of the old Tendai pilgrimage running paths into asphalt roads, marathon monks still ply their way down these routes at predawn hours in their purificatory practices. In the Shugendo sect, practice life is focused on pilgrimage to and ascent of sacred mountains and ceremonial activities in which the mountain is the ground and space for practice.

In Asia, mountains have called pilgrims to them for thousands of years. In the summer of 1987, I hitchhiked across Tibet in order to walk around such a mountain. This mountain you could not climb, and not because of physical obstacles; rather there are sacred laws that have kept its crown free from trespass. For many, many years, pilgrims have made their way to this holy place. They have come from the south, from the dry and wet heat of India. They have come from the east, from the high plains, barley fields, and villages of Tibet. They have come from the grasslands of the north and the deserts of the west as well. They have walked with and against the sun around this mountain. They have been brought as babies to be carried around this mountain, and as elders, they have made their way to this place to die.

Some circle this great body in a day. Others seem to take a lifetime to make the circuit. Some ride on yaks, and others ride the Earth around this holy giant as they prostrate with dust clinging to their bellies. With three friends I walked, just simply walked, one step at a time, around the big four-sided body of this Mountain Being.

In the beginning I thought I was walking around Mount Kailas. I was convinced of it. I looked constantly to my right, and there was its snowy pyramidal crown. Mount Kailas. At the end of the walk, it seemed as though I had circumambulated myself. I somehow was standing outside myself and walking around myself. It was not until some years after the journey that the mountain would disappear into me. But I would have to dream it many times, the joy and suffering of this walk. After this, the mountain would appear inside the atmosphere of my mind.

I had known for twenty-five years about this mountain that I was to encounter and in whose body I was to be given a new body. What took me to Tibet was Buddhist practice, learning from shamans, a profound concern for tribal peoples and the environments in which they live, and the passion I have for wilderness. I was also sent there by one of my Native American teachers, who had told me to go to complete a rite of purification, to offer myself to this place. The pilgrimage had been set in my bones for many years. In a secret way, Tibet and the rare atmosphere of Mount Meru, the mythological name for the great Kailas, begin and end the story of this book.

In the summer of 1987 three traveling companions and I sat around a small pink Formica table in an apartment in Kathmandu. We were guests of Daku Tenzing Norgay. It was tea time, and a visit with Daku had been long overdue. She and I had hiked to the base camp of Kanchenjunga years before, and during that journey we had developed a strong friendship. One night, after a severe snowstorm in the high altitudes of Sikkim, I told her of my commitment to make the

Kailas *perikerama* (circumambulation). Now that promise was going to be fulfilled. Daku wanted to leave her husband's ashes on the Dolma Pass of Kailas and wished to join our party but was not able to because she could not obtain a visa. Her husband, Tenzing Norgay, was the first man to attain the summit of Mount Everest. His life from that moment had taken on superhuman as well as problematic aspects as he suffered both from fame and from alcohol. To take his ashes to Kailas would ensure him an auspicious rebirth.

In the middle of the small pink shiny table beside the teapot were two *tsa-tsa,* miniature stupas made of Tenzing's ashes. Such objects represent the enlightened form of the Buddha. Would I take them to Kailas on her behalf? I carefully wrapped the *tsa-tsa* in red cloth and put them in my pack with the promise that her request would be fulfilled. So began the two months of travel through rain and mud, across great and spacious landscapes, through lifeways of soldiers, lamas, and nomads that brought our little party of four to the Mountain of the Four Directions.

We left Kathmandu valley at the beginning of August and traveled north to the end of the road destroyed by the monsoon. We were lightly geared for two months of travel—food, shelter, and clothing, no more than forty pounds apiece. The point was not to take the West with us but to leave behind as much as possible.

Because of the wild rains, roads had vanished along the winding river's course, cutting off the flow of vehicular traffic between Nepal and Tibet.

It took four days of foot travel to make our way into Tibet. We struggled through living mud slides, dodged falling rocks as cliffs were blasted to open a new road, and made our way with a stream of humanity northward. This was the summer of 1987, and people of every description were drawn to Tibet for a taste of liberation that was to last for only an instant.

Even before we had departed Nepal, as we with great difficulty made our way toward the border, I had begun to question my sanity in undertaking this endeavor. I noticed that those few Westerners who were on the trail were in their twenties, and I began to think that I had exceeded the age limit. But the ashes in my pack would become a companion for me, urging me on when my will weakened. Finally we crossed the border and caught rides in jeeps, trucks, and buses to an army post in the high, purple-and-tan central valley of Tibet.

In the freezing predawn, still aching and confused with altitude sickness, I squeezed into a bus and hoped that the sun would soon rise to reveal the expanse of the country through which we were passing. We had climbed by foot and vehicle close to ten thousand feet in these past few days, and the world of familiar sights and sounds, the world of Western things and thoughts, was just beginning to fade from my consciousness.

North we went to Shigatse, the seat of the Panchen Lama. Carefully avoiding the jaws of hungry dogs, we circled the great monastery of the Panchen Lama and on full moon in August witnessed the most spectacular display of lightning I have ever seen. It was symbolic of the nature of central and western Tibet. Nothing is mediated. Everything seems to strike directly—the penetrating and pervasive light, the relentless wind, the sand from her high deserts that blasts away skin, the great rivers sourced in her that feed and flood the plains of India and China, the directness and humor of the people of the far west that sweeps away one's disquietude, the slap of monks' hands as they triumph in debate, and even the odd and cold cruelty of many of the Chinese colonists who regard Tibet as a savage hell.

I could see why the shamans of the high altitudes had invented a Book of the Dead that then became a map for the Buddhists who were to arrive later. I discovered why oracles and trance mediums found fertile ground in this barren land. I understood why the Mountain of Kailas was holy not only to those who practice the religion of Bon, the indigenous shamanism of Tibet, but also to Hindus, Jains, and Buddhists. For even in the days before the Chinese army made entry and exit to this land difficult, only those with will and good fortune made it through the obstacles impeding access to this aspect of Earth and the mind that it evokes.

Traveling to Lhasa and then south again, I often thought I would just keep on going south back to Nepal, so difficult was the journey. But the ashes in my pack seemed to have a voice of their own, and so I turned west at Lhatse and did the long hard stretch toward Kailas. After two weeks of riding in truck, bus, and jeep, I finally saw the mountain rise behind boiling clouds.

The old bus we were in stopped its tortured movement and disgorged almost all of us. There we stood on the wrinkled ground of a dry riverbed to see the white head of the mountain appear. One could never confuse Kailas with any other mountain. Shaped like a pyramid, its flanks shimmering with snow, it looks from certain angles like a sphinx, silent and mysterious. From its north side, faces appear on its flanks, like guardians, old men, or ancestors. Its west face asks one in, and the eastern face is hidden.

Finally we arrived in Tarchen (altitude 15,100 feet), a small settlement on the south side of Kailas, whose altitude reaches 22,028 feet. We began to set up camp amid cold, chaotic winds coming from every direction. The atmosphere was filled with charged particles, and each thought, each action felt amplified. An argument broke out between me and one of my companions; the tension that had been building between the two of us over these months in Asia blew up in this wild and restless wind. I was exhausted from the journey. My backbone rubbed raw from hard travel, my psychic spine was also painfully exposed. When my companion attacked me, I broke. All of the unexpressed fears about survival rushed to the surface, and suddenly I felt like a Tibetan being beaten by the Chinese. In the midst of this, I thought, I am in Tibet. Who are the Chinese anyway? Who is the enemy anyway? Nearby were lama and Bonpo priest, herder and mother, soldier and pilgrim. Who are we anyway? What's the big deal? We seem so small in this landscape: a dark blue sky above and an endless horizon.

I stayed alone in my tent by the river. Upriver, laundry was being washed and animals' guts cleaned out. The freezing water rushing past my tent seemed pure despite the filth it carried along. Yaks were circling my sleeping place. I remembered the tales of bandits in this region, but one is so exposed here that any protection other than the spiritual kind is useless. Kailas, Shiva's birthplace, Buddha's final resting place, was sheltering all of us who were sleeping and waking in the shadow of a mountain.

It was too early to begin our journey around the mountain. Full moon was several weeks away. Spiritual athletes of every color were doing *nying-kor*, one-day shots around the mountain. The more circumambulations of the mountain, the more merit is generated, according to local tradition. It's a long, hard way to Kailas, so a few heartier and more spiritually ambitious pilgrims did their high-speed, seventeen-hour high-altitude walks with a frequency that daunted this feeble observer.

Most were going in the "Dalai Lama" direction, clockwise. But some went in the "Bon" direction, counterclockwise. Judging by the number of Tibetans going counterclockwise, I have a hunch that the old Bonpo tradition is gaining in strength. Bonpo would make it possible for a believer to work with the difficult circumstances in Tibet through the spirit realm, through magic. Although Tibetan Buddhism is probably one of the most interesting traditions for working with negative forces, the Bon tradition has old, old roots, much older than Buddhism. These years of suffering and oppression that Tibetan people have had to endure under Chinese rule may be fertilizing the roots of the Bon tradition. Certainly, there is evidence of increasing strength in the Bon tradition among Tibetans living in Kathmandu.

South of Kailas is Lake Manasaraovar, fifty-five miles in circumference. Its name means "Lake Born from the Mind of Brahma." Although we had thought only about the mountain, something moved us south to the lake to await the waxing of the moon. We arrived at Chiu Gompa (Bird Monastery), past the gold mines on the Ganga Chu that connects the waters of Manasaraovar with Lake Raksas Tal. The latter is the dark lunar brother to Manasaraovar's sun body. The waters of Lake Manasaraovar seemed to cleanse whatever was offered to them—clothes, dinner dishes, or us, inside and out. They say that immersion in its waters ensures one an incarnation as a god.

I finally went into partial seclusion in a meditation cave high up a cliff on the north side of the lake. From my perch, I watched storms making and unmaking themselves. Light and darkness moved in and out of each other as day passed into night. The great massif, Gurla Mandhata, glistened like a huge, white crouching animal on the opposite shore of the lake. Ravens floated below my cave as I hung in the air on the tiny stone terrace made years ago by the hands of some brave pilgrim. On the blackened ceiling of my cell were the constellations daubed in *tsampa,* roasted barley flour. A stone box lined with freshwater seaweed was my bed. The small altar above my head held a picture of His Holiness the Dalai Lama.

The lake, like Kailas, is a place where circumambulation is made. We had intended to do this, but I was too weak from loss of weight and the strains of the journey to make the trip. We were also almost out of food. A lama who had lived in a nearby cave for three years gave us *tsampa,* wheat flour, and rice to help tide us over. We supplemented this with nettles collected for soup. The Tibetan diet, at this level anyway, is simple, and I related to the ascetic Milarepa's cave practice without too much difficulty.

At last I seemed to be out of earshot of the neurobabble of Western culture. I was convinced that it was the altitude, but one morning I recognized that my receiver was down, and sitting in the cave, I at last knew what it was to be literally stoned, to move at a rate of speed like that of rocks, stones, and mountains. Things were going very slowly. I now understand how a place can shape the human psyche. This vast, clear lake with its wild and barren shore mirrored the ever-changing weather and light of the region. In the stillness of dawn, I looked into the face of Manasaraovar and discovered that my face was also still and empty of "weather." The spirit of this place is big and free. I was caught by its emptiness.

Full moon was less than a week away, and so we left Manasaraovar for Kailas. Back in Tarchen, we wandered among the camped nomads, buying a bit of very rancid yak butter, freshly ground *tsampa*, and sweets. Then one morning, early, before leaving for the *perikerama*, I prepared forty-four *chapatis*, eleven for each of us along the way. Cooking the *tsampa* and flour *chapatis* one by one in the tiny pan top brought me completely into the present moment. This done, we departed with a minimum of gear.

Within a few steps, it was clear to me that I needed to find my own way and my own stride. At first I was behind the others. Then with a burst of energy, I flowed along the trail, leaving behind the sense of the personal. Suddenly, I was at the first Chakstel Gang, one of four prostration stations at the four corners of the mountain. Turning the southwest corner to enter the west valley, I once more looked south and saw Gurla Mandhata and Raksas Tal in the distance and was reminded of the purifying days at the lake. I turned my back on this scene, and walking past piles of carved *mani* stones and yak skulls, prayer flags beating in the wind, I headed north along Kailas's west flank.

The lush green valley, called the Valley of the River of the Gods, has a fine stream meandering through thick mounds of grassy earth. Cushion for at least a dozen pilgrim families, the valley has long been a place of transit for trader and pilgrim alike. Old men and women, newborns, and large families lazed in the warm summer sun, having tea, laughing, and celebrating the commencement of the formal part of the *kora*, the circumambulation. I was invited as I moved along to join this one and that for the inevitable cup of yak butter tea.

Warmed by good company and nourishment, I moved down the trail like a spirit with no sense of hindrance. The great Tarboche (Flagpole) that is dedicated to the Buddha drew me. Pointing toward the heavens, it was woven round with flags in the colors of the five Buddha families. Yak hair and clothing were tied to the stringers that anchor the pole to Earth. At a distance, I saw three old women dressed in black yak-wool *chubas* moving in a circle around the pole. I followed their footsteps as my gaze was drawn to the center pole and then toward the heavens where the sky showed itself an intense, deep blue. Each year, a great *mela* is held when the flagpole is dug out and raised in the early morning of the May full moon, the day of Buddha's birth, enlightenment, and death. As I left the well-trodden path around the pole, I turned toward it one more time and saw it as an exclamation point that marked change.

My companions did not appear, and so on I flew. A wild sense of joy beat on the ground as each step took me northward. The sky was turning darker, and I decided to spend the night alone. I watched the ridges of the western range etch themselves in black on Kailas's west face. The evening light was penetrating, and I walked on to see where I would sleep for the night.

At dark, I came upon a most unusual boulder. It was blackened with soot and shiny with yak butter; many offerings of *mani* stones were on the ground around it. These offering stones, carved with the mantra *Om Mani Padmi Hum* (The Jewel in the Lotus), had been left by the devout. The great rock, called the Saddle of Faith, is a place to pray for an auspicious rebirth, an opportunity I had not anticipated. I carefully laid out my sleeping bag so my head was toward the huge stone and the holy mountain was guarding my feet. Later that night the moon would rise almost full over this place, and I stayed awake and followed its light until dawn.

As it turned out, I had bedded down on the trail. All through the night pilgrims passed by me, and I mentally went with them on their night *kora*. Goat, sheep, and yaks wandered past me just after dark and before rising. Again the utter joy of being in this place sent me shaking. Before the moon came, the sky was washed with stars. After the moon came, the sky was washed with light. At dawn, I moved on.

Although the altitude was 16,000 feet, I felt no shortness of breath. When I reached the north end of the west valley, the sun greeted me. Time for a bath. The ground was thawing, and so was I. Off came the jeans and long underwear, and in I went. What an ecstasy! This was beyond cold.

The walk continued. But shortly I was in the company of two Khampas who kept me flying along the north side of Kailas, where I gestured that I would not go with them over the pass that night. Full moon was the next day. Something needed to be done beneath Kailas's core in the glacial melt. So my Khampa friends and I passed three hours in the making and drinking of tea, and then they disappeared into the afternoon.

I, on the other hand, walked, one breath, one step, toward the core and the north face of Kailas.

Near the top, birds were landing on my shoulders and riding me for steps at a time. I had never been this high before. The next day, two of my companions and I would make this climb again. We bathed the *tsa-tsa* of Tenzing's ashes in the milky glacial waters, purification for Tenzing Norgay's remains. At the core, we left offerings that we had carried for others to this high place and then descended in a snowstorm. That night the sky blazed white with the moon.

Is the point of the pilgrimage the pass, I wondered? And so the four of us, reunited, began the climb, but now our gear was being carried by yaks and we walked in the company of a large Drogpa family, nomads of the region who were also doing the *perikerama*. Halfway to Dolma Pass (the Pass of the Noble Mother Tara), we crossed through Shiwa Tsal, the "Place of Yama," the Lord of Death. Old clothing, human and yak hair, and other offerings were scattered across the rocky landscape. This is the realm of death before rebirth on the pass. The sense of the journey as initiation deepened here when I saw a pilgrim lying as if dead among the scattered offerings. I myself stopped and sat quietly in the midst of old clothing and hair and gazed up at the final ascent to the pass. Birth and rebirth require sacrifice. What is to be sacrificed? What is to be saved?

I stood up and began to walk up the Hill of Salvation one step at a time. Just before we arrived at the pass, a wild snowstorm hit the mountain with relentless energy. The Drogpas, their yaks, and our gear disappeared into flying snow as we neared the summit, and as I arrived at the summit's great stone shrine, wind was howling through its prayer flags, clothing, and yak hair offerings. I remembered that another name for the pass is "The Mother Who Helps One Cross Over." It was time to leave Tenzing's ashes at Tara's great stone shrine.

The feeling of wolf was in the air. Not only was a snowstorm besieging the pass, but one of our party had fallen into a rage. The energy of such places amplifies whatever is in the air. In the midst of atmospheric and psychological changes, I climbed the great icy black shrine, the Dolma Stone, and left the *tsa-tsa* of Tenzing Norgay's ashes on its summit. According to legend, the Noble Mother Tara disappeared beneath this great stone in the form of twenty-one wolves after she helped the monk Gotsangpa get to the top of the pass. The icy stone was carved with mantras, dotted with offerings of frozen yak butter and *tsampa,* and adorned with stringers on which flags, hair, and clothing were flying. All around the frozen, glistening rock were offerings of garments, tea bowls, bags, and sacred stones.

Suddenly, the sky cleared, and we raced through the snow down the other side of the pass. There was no trail, no path. Also there was no warm and dry place to stay in the rainy valley below, so we sang for our supper in the warm tent of our Drogpa companions. This was the east side of Kailas, whose face was now hidden.

The next day the wind took off our skin as we pushed against it toward Tarchen and the end of the *kora*. One discovers during pilgrimage that there is no place to escape from oneself. Whatever the mountain gives you, Earth and Sky give you, you cannot refuse. Pilgrimage is not the mountain, nor the pass. The mountain is a mirror that accurately reflects the minds of those who come to it. Like the circle, which is a sign of nonduality, the walk around Mount Kailas is about the perfection of our true nature in all of its displays.

Although I can say little to nothing about my own true nature, I can say that Kailas took me down and into its depths even as I crossed over its pass. Little was left of me psychically or physically after circling it. Leaving Kailas, the way back to Nepal along the Brahmaputra River across the southern deserts of Tibet was no easier. Whatever I had lost on Kailas, I lost the rest on the journey home.

> The birds have vanished into the sky,
> and now the last cloud drains away.
> We sit together, the mountain and me,
> until only the mountain remains.

Mountain pilgrimages bring the quality of firmness into the life of an individual, a firmness of place and vision that is hard earned. The firmness arises out of the complete physical involvement the mountain demands of the pilgrim. It also confirms the sense of the continuity of things it brings to the journeyer. Born and reborn again, as cloud and river, rock and clay, mountains bring us into the experience of returning to the origins of peoples and of place.

This is certainly true for many Native Americans. Alfonso Ortiz recalls how a mountain for his people is where the Road of Life begins and later where it ends in the transition through death and where a new road begins again.

> One summer a few years ago a man who was, like me, a Tewa Pueblo Indian and I undertook a journey. We were driving to the country of the Utes in southwestern Colorado to share in the blessings of their Sun Dance. My companion had never in his life been in that part of Colorado before. As the massive outcropping that is known today as Chimney Rock loomed larger and larger beyond the road ahead he became very alert. Pointing to it, he said, "There is Fire Mountain! It is just as the old people spoke of it." As he recognized distinct features of the place, he proceeded to unfold tale after tale of events in the early life of our people which took place at Fire Mountain and in the surrounding country. Every prominent feature along the road began to live for him, and as he spoke of that remembered place, we, each of us, began to realize that we were retracing a portion of the ancient journey of our people.

John Muir believed that "going to the mountains is going home." Fire Mountain, a mountain gate of change carried inside the dream of origins, had not been forgotten by Ortiz and his friend although they had never physically visited it. Through a primordial memory, they were carried back in time to a place that they had actually never left, following an ancestral track that confirmed their connection to the past as well as to a place.

The Buddhist realizes that the blue mountain is walking. The Native American hears the blue mountain talking. I have heard mountains sing and mountains shake with the power of thunder. Mountains whistle with the power of wind and whisper with pine. Mountains crackle, groan, and roar with glacial energies. And mountains hold their silence in stillness, like great meditators abiding at the edge of the horizon. Mountains also mark the boundaries of the known world. The Dineh count their origins east of the center of four sacred mountains.

I have often visited this place, still known as Dineh Tah, or "Among the People." It is high country with endless, changing skies, turning canyons, wild rock, and a landscape of fragrant piñon and juniper. The old ones say that during the time before time, First Man and First Woman, Changing Woman, and her sons Monster Slayer and Child Born of Water lived there. First Man and First Woman lived near the Central Mountain, the Mountain Around Which Everything Turns. They discovered Changing Woman on the summit of nearby Gobernador Knob. Her children, Monster Slayer and Child Born of Water, eventually came home to the central place of

Huerfano Mountain after killing the monsters that troubled the world at that time. Today Dineh people still herd their sheep, hunt, and pray in this elemental land guarded by these same sacred mountains.

The Dineh say that no worlds can be conceived of in the past, present, or future without the arrangement and activities of mountains. Mountains anchor and articulate all elements of the universe. They are connected to, fastened to, and covered with elements of the natural world, including stones, day skies, jewels, birds, vegetation, sound, inhabitants, the power of motion, and special gifts and geological features. Mountains are said to represent parts of the Earth's body, and like our bodies, they have the power of motion initiated by the Holy Wind. According to the Dineh, "these [sacred] mountains are our father and our mother. We came from them; we depend upon them. Between the large mountains are small ones which we made ourselves. Each mountain is a person. The water courses are their veins and arteries. The water in them is their life as our blood is to our bodies."

Mountains for the Dineh have an outer, inner, and secret form. In their outer form, mountains are mountains whose physical bodies generate rain and other living substances. Their inner bodies are the abodes of Holy Beings. Mountains are Holy People and guardians of the Dineh world. Their secret forms live inside the human being and are realized only by knowing directly their outer and inner forms. This secret mountain is both visible and invisible to the human eye. One can see it living in the creases of a man's face or hear it in the ringing strength of a woman's voice. It lives in the human heart of wisdom and compassion. It lives in the enlightened activity of storyteller and healer, tree planter and carver, farmer and singer. It lives in the human respect for mountains and all terrains.

Within and around the earth,
within and around the hills,
within and around the mountains,
your authority returns to you.

The true nature of mountains is that they are mountains. They practice both stillness holding their place and moving with change. Men and women can be reborn through mountains. Ancestors abide in mountains. And mountains disappear the closer you are to them. As Dogen wrote in the *Shobogenzo*: "They passed eons living alone in the mountains and forests; only then did they unite with the Way and use mountains and rivers for words, raise the wind and rain for a tongue, and explain the great void." Realizing fully the true nature of place is to talk its language and hold its silence.

Why climb a mountain?
Look! a mountain there.
I don't climb mountain.
Mountain climbs me.
Mountain is myself.
I climb on myself.
There is no mountain
nor myself.
Something moves up and down
in the air.

Nanao Sakaki

5

The Way of Language

Demon or bird! (said the boy's soul),
Is it indeed toward your mate you sing?
or is it really to me?
For I, that was a child, my tongue's use sleeping,
how I have heard you,
Now in a moment I know what I am for, I awake,
And already a thousand singers, a thousand songs,
clearer and louder and more sorrowful than yours,
A thousand warbling echoes have started to live
with me, never to die.
> Walt Whitman, "Out of the Cradle
> Endlessly Rocking"

Will we talk to mountains and clouds, I ask myself, as our ancestors did? Will we ask the oak whether we should plant a garden near it? Can we hear the voice of the stones in the sweat lodge? Can we hear salmon asking us to protect and restore their rivers? Do we understand what owl tells us in the dark of night, or what the clouds say in their silent script? Can we hear the sounds of the world, like Kuan-yin, the Buddhist goddess of compassion?

One's identity expands inside the bodies of minerals, plants, animals, and elements as well as inside the subtle world of ancestors and spirits. Speaking in creation's tongues, hearing creation's voices, the boundary of our soul expands. Earth has many, many voices. Those who understand that Earth is a living being know this because they have translated themselves to the humble grasses and old trees. They know that Earth is a community that is constantly talking to itself, a communicating universe, and whether we know it or not, we are participating in the web of this community. A Dineh man remembered the advice of his grandfather: "Know that things in nature are like a person. Talk to tornadoes; talk to the thunder. They are your friends and will protect you."

I learned from the late Dineh elder Gray Whiskers that the medicine people in his culture use the sounds that are woven into the name of an object to evoke the power of that which is named. The Dineh understand that all beings, be they star or stone, are condensations of sound, solidified vibration. To connect with the medicine, or power, of lightning and star, one must sound them. Medicine singers of the Dineh use chants as keys to open the mysteries of seemingly unpredictable and uncontrollable nature. The singer of the Shooting Star Chant knows the language of lightning. The singer of the Windway can call wind. The Mountain Chant singer knows the language of mountains. The singer is a specialist who through knowledge of evocative language has access to the natural world. There is a "Twelve-Word Song of Blessing," sung by the Dineh, which is a song of power, each word opening a world:

Earth
Sky
Mountain Woman
Water Woman
Talking God
xactceoyan
Boy-carrying-single-corn-kernel
Girl-carrying-single-turquoise
White-corn-boy
Yellow-corn-girl
Pollen Boy
Cornbeetle Girl

Among the Dineh, the word *nílch'i* means wind, atmosphere, air. *Nílch'i* is not only found in our common atmosphere. It is also present in motion, in the life force, in thought, and in speech, the turning of the word. *Nílch'i,* translated "Holy Wind," is the body that carries the messages of all beings to one another, including plants, animals, features of the Earth, the stars and planets, all of whom are alive. As these natural beings are gifted with Holy Wind and the inner forms with which to think, they are able to instruct and guide human beings in how to live on Earth. A Dineh puts it this way:

> The one called Holy Wind and Wind [*alilee naaghaii*]
> stands within us.
> The same one turns that one that walks about [the Sky?], I say.
> It turns this [earth], I say.
> It turns water, everything.

It alone is our Holy One.
Really, only it is our prayer.

According to the Dineh, it is through this Holy Wind that the world came into being. For from the Wind came the Word. The vibrations of words solidified into phenomena. Thus all things are related through the Holy Wind and the Word.

Thomas Berry, in *The Dream of the Earth,* has said that most of us suffer from a kind of autism when it comes to communicating with anything other than our own kind. The Holy Wind has been stilled within our lives, and we live in a cultural atmosphere that does not confirm the mutuality of creation. Even when we recognize our kinship and intimacy with other forms of existence, we remain mute before them. Their language has been forgotten. We are enclosed in a psychocultural cocoon; the outer world no longer flows into our being. Those voices remain unheard, and we are unable to speak in response. The winds of communication with creation are dying. Yet Earth and language meet and metabolize in the zones of dream and visions, in story, poetry, song, and prayer, and in direct communion with untamed beings. These zones comprise the boundary lands where cultural constraints and social habits are overridden, where tribal folk, shamans, and children, the mad and inspired, are caught in the holy wind of creation.

Tribal peoples and their shamans have much to teach us about the language of the Earth. Shamans have the gift of speaking with beings in nonhuman realms, and many tribal folk talk to the world around them as a good friend. Not oversentimental, the Swampy Cree Isaac Greys says this to the blue jay:

> Old jay, loudmouth of the tree!
> Tell me the news.

For shamans, this gift develops through the initiation crisis, the crisis that takes them out of the social realm into chaotic, unstructured zones that are open-ended, often terrifying, yet rich with possibilities. In this liminal condition, the neophyte shaman becomes vulnerable and receptive to communication with spirits and animals.

This is "the kiss of knowledge," the experience of intimacy with the nonhuman world. Such communion with plants, creatures, geographical features, and the unseen can involve language or be beyond words altogether. The process of transmission between shaman and Other is portrayed in the Raven's Rattle of the Kwá kwaka'wakw, an indigenous group of the Northwest Coast who carve the shaman in a reclining position with his or her tongue entering the mouth of a frog or another being. Shamans develop this ability for magical and healing speech by surrendering to that which attacks them. By being receptive to their enemy, they receive the medicine of their adversary. In this way, the enemy becomes their ally, be it lightning, storm, wild waters, eagle, or bear.

Many children can communicate with nonhumans without the mediation of crisis. One afternoon in Thich Nhat Hanh's Plum Village in southern France, a very young Vietnamese boy said he had to talk with me. He had heard that I could talk to stones. I answered, "Yes, sometimes I am able to converse with rocks and stones, but not all the time." I then asked him how he had learned about this, and he replied, "The stones told me."

Shamans and children use languages that differ from the language of everyday life. They can speak in the tongues of Others and enter the language of beasts, spirits, ancestors, elements, and environmental features. Dogen Zenji said that not all things speak with a human tongue. Clearly, if we are to become the sum of all our relations, then what is needed is an ability to speak the languages of creation.

We humans have many language alternatives available to us. There are languages reserved for ritual occasions. There is communication through the use of vocables, "nonsense" syllables that carry the feeling of what is being said. There is the language the shaman enters that is used by another species, like speaking in the tongue of wolf. Then there is communication beyond language altogether, beyond words and sounds—direct communication, or communion in the body of silence.

Languages reserved for sacred occasions include Latin for Catholics and Sanskrit for Buddhists. A contemporary example of a language now being used for sacred occasions is Lakota. Although there are many native Lakota speakers, many non-Lakota people use Lakota phrases when they smoke the Chanunpa (sacred pipe) or pray in the Stone People Lodge. In this case, a language of one group of tribal peoples is being adopted by other peoples as a sacred language.

Grandfather Wallace Black Elk notes that Sanskrit and Latin, the roots of many of our Western contemporary languages, are dead. The Lakota language, however, is still alive, its roots drawing nourishment from the Earth. Lakota is a language of the North American continent and is flourishing in its native soil. Because of this, according to Grandfather Wallace, it has the power to heal directly. Like the Lakota, the Shoshone say that their language "is rooted in the song of the Earth." The Northern Ute say that the "voice of the land is in our language." They still thrive in the body of the Earth.

For the most part, words in sacred languages have retained their meaning. But there are many instances in which the sounds that are sung or prayed with in tribal cultures seem to have no meaning in the conventional sense. At the Cantometrics Project at Columbia, when we looked at a song text that was composed of only vocables, we would call them "nonsense syllables." Later, I realized that they were not nonsensical at all. Such songs are filled with meaning in the way that they are sung. Here is part of a Dineh coyote chant from the Enemy Way: *"heya heya heya.a ho.ho. yaha hahe.ya.an."*

When the Dineh scholar Father Berard Haile asked for the meaning of the song, he was told,

"The words have no meaning, but the song means, 'Take it, I give it to you.'"

There are also vocables that are invented when two parties actively create a third language unique to a particular occasion. Allen Ginsberg once told me about an experience he had in Japan in which improvisation and language met in the creation of a third language of meaning. He encountered a group of Japanese poets, none of whom spoke English, and Ginsberg knew little Japanese. The group entered the space of a third and new language. This language was not a language of logic but a language of sensing and intuition. It had color, tonality, and cadence whose source was in the imagination. It was a language of vocables that were co-created and thus the glue that held together this communication between contraries (or poets).

Vocables are about sound and breath. They are a kind of spell, what the anthropologist Bronislav Malinowski has called "the coefficient of weirdness," that unites the singer and the beings around him or her into a bond of power that is far beyond the human realm. The poet Jerome Rothenberg notes that vocables can be purely invented and meaningless sounds, distortions of ordinary words and syntax, ancient words emptied of their meaning, or words that are borrowed from other languages. These vocables can be explained as spirit language, animal language, or a language of the ancestors.

Other kinds of vocables are those used by shamans who can speak wolf or whale. By stepping out of the timespace of culture and entering a zone transcending social forms or social conventions, the shaman practices exchanging self with other. Vicente Huidobro, the Chilean poet, puts it this way:

> I'm the mad cosmic
> Stones plants mountains
> Greet me Bees rats
> Lions and eagles
> Stars twilights dawn
> Rivers and jungles all ask me
> What's new How you doing?
> And while stars and waves have something
>   to say
> It's through my mouth they'll say it

I like it that Huidobro uses stars and waves as a vehicle of communication. True to tribal people, the Binga of Gabon do it as the creatures do it:

> The fish does . . . HIP
> The bird does . . . VISS
> The marmot does . . . GNAN

This identification with another being reveals the world from the view of the fish, bird, or marmot, yet it is more than a simple process of identification. The shaman actually feels as though he or she is in the body of the other being and speaks its language through its body. This wonderful ability is a kind of transubstantiation—a transformation of consciousness from body to body through the vehicle of language. One day when the anthropologist Frances Harwood and I were discussing the shaman's gift of shifting shapes, she noted that doctors give out medicine, whereas shamans *are* medicine. In other words, shamans get all mixed up with creation and do not hold themselves apart from life but rather are consumed by it. In this way, they become medicine itself. Another important point.

The ground of all these forms of communication is silence, a way that creation is known that is beyond words altogether. We might call it communion. It is direct knowing, direct sensing, and direct understanding.

What is this silence that lies behind language? And what is the relationship between language and silence? One way of looking at nonduality (and healing) is in terms of silence and language. The power of silence should not be underestimated. Nor should the power of words. Language shapes silence; it gives silence rhythm, pitch, and texture. When words become embodied in beings, they become the ornaments and reminders of silence. Silence is the ground. Language and words bring "things" into "being" out of the ground of emptiness. What carries the Word is breath. In the beginning, say the Dineh, was the Holy Wind. And from the Holy Wind came the Word. Words are Spirit transmuted into substance. According to the Dineh, they make our relationships not only substantial but also beautiful, and the act of ritual speech establishes order and harmony in the world. Without holy speech, the boundaries of the world shrink, and humans are left in a wasteland outside the web of great nature. Without silence, we cannot hear the voices of all beings.

Like silence, shared language is a sign of common understanding. For tribal peoples, each being has its own language. For the Lakota, the sacred pipe is a way to communicate with all beings and is similar to a transformer making the currents of differing languages comprehensible. The Chanunpa amplifies holy wind in the act of smoking. Through it we can hear the voices of creation, and our prayers can be heard by creation. This act of listening closely to the world helps us see the rich net of relationships in which we are embedded. Hermann Hesse wrote,

> Sometimes, when a bird cries out,
> Or the wind sweeps through a tree,
> Or a dog howls in a far-off farm,
> I hold still and listen for a long time.
>
> My soul turns and goes back to the place
> Where, a thousand forgotten years ago,
> The bird and the blowing wind
> Were like me, and were my brothers.
>
> My soul turns into a tree,
> And an animal, and a cloud bank.
> Then changed and odd it comes home
> And asks me questions. What should I
>   reply?

Clearly one of the ways we can heal the perception that we are separate from each other is through language (and shared silence). The sacred languages used during ceremony or evoked in various states of consciousness outside culture (if we are Westerners) can move teller, singer, and listener out of the habitual patterns of perception. Indeed, speaking in the tongues of sea and stone, bird and beast, or moving beyond language itself is a form of perceptual healing.

In exploring perceptual healing over the years, I have often speculated on how the specifics of language, especially a sacred language shared by shamans in a particular society, might also be understood by people outside the culture. In the mid-seventies, a friend and I asked Don José and a group of students to participate in an informal experiment. It was our contention that the words and tonalities Don José used in his chants directly evoked the images about which he was chanting. Don José sang a short chant for a group of twenty students. He then repeated the chant phrase by phrase, and the group gave their impressions of what he was singing about. The correspondence between the content of the Huichol chant and the listeners' images was very high indeed.

Don José, like many other medicine people, had the uncanny ability to transmit sensations and feelings through language in the context of ceremony. Certainly the Mazatec shaman Maria Sabina, who spoke for the mushrooms, had this gift. And once, when I was listening to Joe David sing in the Nuu-Chal-Nulth language, I saw his face transform for an instant into an eagle. As it turned out, the song he was giving me was from this great bird. The power of language, the force of words shape the landscapes of our minds. The landscapes of our minds shape our environment. The world around us, culture and the wilderness, make indelible impressions on our minds. A time-less conversation is going on among all things, yet we seem to have selected out our next of kin as the only ones we actually listen to.

Once I asked Don José what it was like during the old time of paradise when all species could communicate with one another. The old man laughed and said, "Anything could happen, and you didn't die from it!" I remembered those words when spending time with orcas years ago. For two summers I traveled to Campbell River in British Columbia and boated south to a deserted island on the east side of Johnstone Strait, where I joined a group of friends who were doing research on interspecies communication. The musician Jim Nollman and educator Gigi Coyle had organized this ad hoc summer community to create an environment in which humans and whales could inter-act with each other through the language of music. This was a pretty unusual way to encounter an-other species, not at all like the science I had known at the University of Miami School of Medicine or the Lerner Lab in Bimini. This was more like an interspecies community where time was not structured and the whales called the shots.

During my first summer there, the whales were very active. Although they spent most of their time in Johnstone Bight, we chose not to approach them in their home waters. If they should wish to encounter us, they knew right where we were. To my great surprise they came almost every night in large numbers, whistling and calling in response to our voices, electric guitars, violins, and pianos.

At first I was sure that they came over to our side of the strait because they enjoyed dinner music. But within a week, the whales and our group definitely began to sing together. Voices, guitar riffs, and violin crescendos were broadcast by large underwater amplifiers beneath our research vessel, and the songs of these huge cetaceans reached us through underwater microphones. My doubts about the whales' interest in us were beginning to fade after a few late nights of surprised listening. They ceased altogether when I finally generated sufficient courage to embark in a three-person kayak with Linda Tellington-Jones and David Chary.

Never having been in a kayak before, I was convinced that I would end up in these freezing northern waters. Preoccupied, I hadn't given much thought to whales until we found ourselves at moonless midnight suddenly in a pod of forty orcas, who rose up from the depths with us in their midst. At that moment my body turned to jelly, and I seemed to have lost all my bones. "What if one of these creatures should miscalculate and do us in?" I wildly asked myself. My knees began to dance by themselves, turning the kayak into a drum.

In the meantime, my two companions were busy singing with them. I was very relieved when the whales finally moved past us and we paddled toward shore. The scale of the whale is something I hadn't fully anticipated. Hearing them while comfortably tucked into a sleeping bag on the shore is one thing; being in their midst, and re-membering that you are lower on the food chain, is quite another.

Crawling into my tent, I felt quite small and was thoroughly awake. Memories flooded me like dark water, memories of birth, blindness and paralysis from a childhood illness, car accidents and surgeries, mountain climbing, making love, sitting *zazen*—all memories carried in the breath and the body. Throughout the night I could hear the whales breach in the nearby water.

From the northern polar regions to the south-ern shores of the Americas, interspecies communi-cation between whales and people has a long tradition. For indigenous peoples, whales are linked with life and death and the world between. Whales, like buffalo, provided coastal peoples with food, oil, tools and weapons, clothing, and hous-ing. Whale hunting was dangerous, and the cere-monial life of tribal whalers was intricate and complex, involving initiation rites, ritual proce-dures, and the keeping of many taboos. Nytom, a Makah artist from northwest Washington state, told me years ago that the old whalers of his village used to walk on the backs of the whales as they harpooned them. In fact, whale hunting was a shamanic practice involving the intimacies and exchanges of birth and death.

Although I did not aspire to acquire "whale power," I did not say no to the suggestion that I go into the channel by kayak the next night. And indeed, that evening I found myself in a single kayak, paddling into the night with a group of human companions. After several long meetings about the well-being of the Tibetan monks who were accompanying us and could not swim, His Holiness Tai Situ Rinpoche and Gegen-la were placed in the triple kayak. Gigi, Linda, and I (the quick study) were in singles. Each one of us had a transistor radio and so could hear the interaction between the musicians on our research vessel and the whales in the deep water.

A pod could be heard coming from across the channel heading for the research vessel. The next thing I knew, however, we were in their midst. At this moment of truth, we no longer needed the radios. The Rinpoche sang mantras to them, and Linda and I sang "whale" to them, and they were singing right back, no amplification needed. This was live! Then a giant orca slowly rose out of the depths between three of our kayaks, her great body shimmering with phosphorescence in the moonless night. I was struck with more than a little respect as she slid almost soundlessly back into the water less than fifteen feet from us. The night's finale was a mother whale and baby whistling and growling within touching distance. Although both Linda and I were shaken by the closeness to these creatures, our voices inter-locked with theirs in an interspecies antiphony.

Paddling back to shore in silence, I tried to understand what such an encounter might mean to the whales and what it meant to us humans. Did we look like an indigestible dinner, or new friends? Were they curious about us? What were they doing with us anyway? Meeting creatures in the wild is a powerful experience. It awakens that bittersweet nostalgia for a time when all creatures spoke together and were held in the common em-brace of creatureliness. It also stirs up the stuff of trust when encountering a being who is quite ca-pable of eating you for dinner and doesn't. Then there is the simple wonder of it all. I have had close contact and even communication with snakes, lizards, jays and hawks, dolphins, and coyotes, but whales cannot help but awaken in us the sense of being part of the great natural *sangha,* the community of all creation. Indeed these old beings are our companions in awakening. Strange how some of them seem to seek out the human species. I ask, What is going on here?

I remember a story told to me years ago by Grandfather Semu Huaute, a Chumash elder. When I was about to leave for Point Sal, a coastal wilderness area north of Santa Barbara, he told me that many, many years ago near Point Sal the bears and humans were good friends. "You know, daughter, before the Spaniards came to California, the bears and us used to gather berries together. The bears were real friendly. We got along real well. We could talk to each other, and we had a good understanding. When the Spaniards came, they found it pretty easy to shoot the bears. After that, the bears wouldn't go berrying with us anymore." The California Yuki poet William Oandasan puts it this way:

long ago brown bears
sang around our lodge fires
tonight they dance
alive through our dreams

Tribal peoples are natural experts in inter-species communication. Today, scientific expertise is brought to bear in exploring its various forms. Music, body contact, computer interface languages, visual languages have all been used as ways to bridge the gap between "us" and "them." But the problem with science is that it is a one-way street where the beings scientists are studying are objectified and can't be seen gazing back at them. Shamans and tribal peoples have carried on their form of two-way interspecies communication for thousands of years. It was important for them to have good relationships with the animals who provided them with food, clothing, housing, and power.

To phase into an exchange with another species there needs to be a different sense of time and space, of atmosphere and environment. This kind of phase shift is reflected in the fine detail and elegance of the animal beings painted on the walls and ceiling of the great Paleolithic initiatory caves in the Dordogne. The portrayal of these animals surely must have been rooted in a relationship of deep intimacy and respect.

It is quite a leap for some Westerners to listen beyond themselves to another species, but this is a good way to practice yielding. Many times I have found myself sitting with an elder who speaks for hours in a language totally unfamiliar to me, and yet the pictures come, and the energy of Presence holds the time together like a well-woven basket. The same happens in the stillness of the desert when I spend days alone listening through the silence to the voices present in that world. Each being has a story that wants to be told, that wants to be heard.

The true language of these worlds opens from the heart of a story that is being shared between species. For us to be restored to the fabric of this Earth, we are bidden to enter this tale once again through its many modes of telling, to listen through the ears of others to the mystery of creation, with its continually changing patterns, and to take part once again in the integral weave of the narrative. Might we not hear our true names if we learn to listen through the ears of Others? Through language, one can exchange one's self with other beings and in this way establish an ever-widening circle of existence.

Spirit that hears each one of us,
hear all that is—
Listens, listens, hears us out—
Inspire us now!
Our own pulse beats in every stranger's
    throat,
And also within the flowered ground
    beneath our feet,
And—teach us to listen!—
We can hear it in water, in wood, and even
    in stone.
We are earth of this earth, and we are bone
    of this bone.
This is a prayer I sing, for we
have forgotten this and so
the earth is perishing.

                    Barbara Deming

6

The Way of Story

The story of my people
and the story of this place
are one single story.
No man can think of us
without thinking of this place.
We are always joined together.
                    A Taos Pueblo Indian man

Are we cut off by our culture from the touch of sacred language? Not entirely, for in the old stories that we tell children, those they tell one another, or the stories and myths we hear told by the elders from tribal cultures, there still vibrate the echoes of our relatedness. Story telling is the most ancient form of education. It is about the remembering, making, and sharing of images that bind together time, nature, and a people. Stories, like the sacred plants, are medicine and food come from the Earth. They remind us that we do not stand alone. Through them we live in the body of coyote and crow, tree and stone, gods and heroes, Ancestral Mothers and Grandmothers. In this way, we confirm our relationship with all of creation. "In the continuance of the stories and songs—the Earth shall continue," said the Pueblo poet Simon

Ortiz. Earth can continue both by being exposed by story and by being protected by story.

Yes, stories are also protectors. Like our immune systems, they defend us and the people against attacks of debilitating alienation. My good friend Steven Foster says that people erect symbolic stories around themselves like houses. These stories are "circles of protection and purpose that bodily carry our spirits all the way to the gates of death." For stories and myths are the connective tissue between culture and nature, between self and other, between life and death that sew the worlds together in their telling. And in the protective and connective body of story the soul quickens. It comes alive.

Maria Chona, a Papago, once said, "My father went on talking to me in a very low voice. This is how our people always talk to their children, so low and quiet, the child thinks he is dreaming. But he never forgets." Her words came to mind when listening to Grandfather Leon Shenandoah, the Tadodaho of the Iroquois Confederacy. I heard him tell the story of how the prophet named the Peacemaker and his lieutenant, Ayawentha, or "He Who Makes Rivers," helped to create the League of Nations, now known as the Six Nations Iroquois Confederacy.

Sitting in a chair, Grandfather Leon's quiet voice takes us into the deep flowing tides of stories and myths that have been heard by his people for many generations. When we listen, at first we try to hold onto the particulars. But we cannot. Even his eyes are closed as he dreams in our midst. Our eyes closed, we can see the old council fires of his people, see the faces in their light. We can see the stars that were their calendars "until white men took the people's stars away." We hear him say of the creatures and his people, "You call the animals wild, but they weren't really wild. They're free. The same with us. We weren't wild. We were free. If we had been wild, Columbus wouldn't have gotten off this island alive." He laughs softly.

And we feel the original Tadodaho, whose hair was made of snakes. Long, long ago, according to Grandfather, this Onondaga wizard was finally persuaded to join the Confederacy. Joining it, he, the greatest enemy of the tribes, was made its chief. Two hundred Tadodahos later, Grandfather Shenandoah reminds us of what went before him and what we are facing in our future. He then repeats the Peacemaker's words: "Think not forever of yourselves, O Chiefs, nor of your own generation. Think of continuing generations of our families; think of our grandchildren and of those yet unborn, whose faces are coming from beneath the ground." Grandfather Leon says that those "faces coming from beneath the ground" can be restored to the Earth through story.

Hearing of myth and story is how we are initiated into the traditions and truths of culture and nature. They prepare us for the future and guide us in the present. Facts and facticity aren't enough. Gregory Bateson once said, "If the world be connected . . . then thinking in terms of stories must be shared by all mind or minds, whether

ours or those of redwood forests and sea anem-
ones." We hear the stories, and what the stories
are about hears the story through us, like the
salmon's story, which turns our hearts and hands
to the fate of northern rivers. We need stories to
make clear the relationships that exist between
the mind of the forest and the mind of the city, the
mind of the river and the human heart. We act on
and in terms of those relationships.

When I was a child, full of anticipation, I
would shake in my grandmother's arms as she
held me in the warm Savannah nights and told me
stories of the spirits that frequented her house. I
could hear them knocking on the walls, and I saw
their ephemeral traces for many years. She also
told me stories about her childhood and youth, a
time when life was lived at a walking pace. It was
these nocturnal tellings, in fact, that set my imagination free. For through her, I began to see that
the so-called inanimate world really had soul and
that another way of seeing and understanding was
possible, lessons that stand inside me to this day.

If learning happens directly through experience and, as I have suggested, indirectly through
language, then how do myth, song, story, and
prayer function as initiation? Reading collections
of mythologies and folktales is not necessarily
going to help us understand how these stories of
beginnings and endings function as the thread
that holds together the cloth of culture with the
fabric of nature. I know that tellings need to unfold in the context of real events in Earth time as
well as dream time.

They are heard by the ear and smelled in the fire's smoke. They can happen in the course of conversation as well as in the process of initiation. Stories knit together the realities of past and future, of dreamed and intended moments. They teach us how we perceive and why we wonder. They lead us to a view of ourselves in relation to the Earth and our ancestors that confirms the continuum of all existence. The stream of life quickens in the story body, and this stream flows through the body of initiation.

Someone long ago told me that Virginia Woolf looked into her dustpan for the stuff of her stories. Stories in the world of tribal peoples find their content in ordinary events that are part of daily life activities as well as in the dream. There seem to be five main informing streams that feed the river of story: the particularities of place, the ancestral continuity, the occasion of its telling, the soul of the teller, and the listener.

Every story I have heard over the many years that I have listened to the tellings of young and old tribal peoples has evoked a terrain and atmosphere that was tangible, that was earthbound. For Earth Peoples, real nature—storm and rushing waters, the silence of winter nights, and the greatness of protecting mountains—makes the story immediate and memorable, coded in geography and in the temper of the seasons. Stories like these are ecology. They make the landscape of the mind and the outer landscape one, thus protecting and enriching both. Weaving together weather and geological features, the particularities of place, into the fabric of story gives the telling strength and truth. It is a way to establish substantiality in that which is timeless. It gives the journey of initiation a real landscape through which it can forever be remembered. In fact, story is one way in which we are initiated into a spiritual relationship with Earth.

Listening to tribal peoples' stories over the years, I have learned that Earth becomes a kind of mirror of the human psyche, and the natural features of a story often refer to the quality of the human unconscious that is explored in the telling. Animals, natural objects and systems, and the world of spirits are also often seen as mirrors of the human world. They can carry the burden of the thoughts and feelings of the social realm just as the language of society can have hidden within it the voices of rock and wind, creature and ancestor.

Stories also need to be told and retold. They are like a path in the forest that becomes your walk only after passing its way many times. Although we humans tend to resist change, the story finally convinces us to yield to the inevitable. Stories are medicine because they teach us about and prepare us for the experience of changing: our mothers prepare us for the social order in the stories they tell us, and the medicine person prepares us for the cosmic order, with its disorder, through his or her stories. The narratives of initiation and of journey and threshold experiences push us out of the social fabric into the fabric of the wilderness and unimpeded space. There we learn that if we want to change our lives, we have to change our stories, stories that contain the lessons for moving past the stuff of collective adaptation.

Tellings also confirm the ancestral continuity. When my grandmother storied me, I could feel her grandmother storying her. I could hear the voices of generations of women from the Southern United States and the British Isles in my grandmother's tales. And when the shaman Don José gave the story of the first *mara'akáme,* Tatewarí—known to us as Our Grandfather Fire—the fire danced at his feet, and I could also see Tatewarí in the old man's eyes, the fire in his soul, his life energy force expressed as this primordial shaman.

I believe that story telling is one of the most important ways that we do the ancestral work that will reconcile us to Earth and Earth Peoples, to our true nature and unimpeded mind. The clear and confused signatures of our ancestors live inside our psyches. Most of us have not seen the personal legacy of those who have gone before, how some of us carry the sorrow of our mothers and their mothers, how hidden within some of us are the ambitions and aspirations of our fathers and their fathers. Ancestral codes shape how we go in the world. We are in the stream of our ancestors, and story can make that stream visible and conscious. Intentionally entering the ancestral stream means entering the darkness, entering the realm of the dead. It means going inward, seeking initiation. Like the wild gander, who has realized the worlds of past, present, and future, the body of story can reconcile these realms in our lives at this very moment.

There is a reason why such stories are most often told in the dark of night. Parents read children stories at bedtime not just to put them to sleep but to awaken the nondiscursive mind. In Hopi communities, after work in the cornfield all day, when the evening meal is done, tobacco is smoked and the story is told in another kind of light.

For me, the smell of wood smoke calls forth stories of many shapes and colors. I have gazed into small fires in Africa, Asia, and the Americas and watched a world unfold in their mutable bodies. I also remember Chan K'in Viejo launching into his round of myths at all hours of the day—morning, afternoon, anytime the ears were there to listen. Sitting in the godhouse, he gestured through us to visible and invisible terrains in the coursing of his story. I learned from this old man that whenever and wherever stories are told, a deeper landscape—the reality behind the reality—can appear.

The shadows of Western culture are expressed in our story box, the television set, but the smell of smoke and the bite of imagination are not there. At the Ojai Foundation, I often watched the faces of those who sat in the kiva staring at the fire. Whereas fire ignites imagination, television robs us of the gift that connects us to Earth and Spirit. Imagination is the source of story and is fed by story. Without imagination, we cannot penetrate our psyches, nor will we allow ourselves to be absorbed by the world around us.

As I write these words, I am looking at a great blue heron who is building a nest in the pine tree next to my father's home. Every once in a while she stretches her long neck and points her head toward the heavens, and I feel the stretch in my throat. She stands immobile for long periods staring into the eastern horizon and then floats to the canal below for some food. I have seen this heron mother for years in the same pine tree. Winter is her season to nest. She stands like a blue-gray guardian of the past, not seeming to take notice of the flow of traffic on the highway to her south. She, like the gander, carries the medicine of the three times and, like the gander, she is one who draws nourishment from the depths.

This great heron reminds me that storying is a kind of root medicine, a way for us to enter our depths and derive nourishment from the fruitful darkness. For her life to succeed, this big mother heron needs her old pine tree and her dark inland water. She needs continuity, heights, and depths for her life to be complete. It is this way with tellings, with stories, with myths, with prayer, prophecy, and song. They call forth the firmness of the tree and the yielding of deep water in moments of transmitted inspiration.

Yes, stories are threads that draw one back into the fabric of the Earth. Bright fibers that join worlds, stories illumine our deep past and our origins, our ancestors and the ancestors of all creation, and our psyches and societies. They also draw us through the eye of the future. There are stories of beginnings, stories that reflect our lives as they are presently lived, and stories about the coming time. Today the prophecies being told by our elder brothers and sisters from tribal cultures teach us that the past, present, and future are connected in the same way that all of creation is connected. Used by cultures and peoples to regulate themselves, prophecies help a people to measure and understand their past and present and to see what might happen in the future based on present human activity.

Many tribal peoples believe that the Earth is perishing because the sacred ways of their cultures are dying or lost. These traditions have kept the world in balance, have protected the Earth through prayer, story, and sacred activity. A Hopi elder, Grandfather David Monongye, said,

> It was foretold that in time the native people would stray from their original path, adopting foreign concepts. Their religious and spiritual values would be demolished, including the foundation. Their language, their culture and their identity will cease to exist. When this happens, a few remnants will remain who are possessed of the wisdom and knowledge of old. If they are fortunate enough, these few will gather together and put together the ancient knowledge which they remember, and go forth in search of the roots the Hopi laid out, until they find the master root. . . . But if these last remnants of the ancient way are toppled, a very great purification by the forces of nature will be called for, in order to restore the plan of the Creator.

Over the years, prophecies have been shared with me by three tribal peoples—Dineh, Lacandon, and Hopi. Each time I listened to elders tell the story of prophecy, I felt as though I were crossing a bridge to another world. On one side of the bridge were towns and cities, factories and schools, highways and automobiles. On the other side was a pathless wilderness where the past, present, and future could be clearly seen. The three elder brothers who told these prophecies—Gray Whiskers, Chan K'in Viejo, and James Kootshongsie—had stepped briefly out of their worlds and opened the gates that keep their peoples free from trespass by those who do not understand that the traditions of aboriginal peoples protect the Earth.

When I listened to these stories, I felt that the communication was taking place between the worlds of human and ancestor, gods and humans, nature and culture. The hand that reached across the bridge that connects these worlds took many forms: it was transparent; it was old and worn; it was animal-like; it was a spirit hand, a sky hand; it was the precious turquoise hand of respect. My hand opened to these gestures of grace.

Prophecies arise from a people's experience of the cycle of the seasons, the cycle of time, the connection with the growing and harvesting of grain, the blooming and dying of flowers, the ripening of fruit, the migration of creatures and heavenly bodies. Time in these worlds has a long body of continuity, sometimes centuries or millennia, and thus frees people from a time-pressured world. When

113

the constancy of the flow of time is shattered by disruptive forces, then prophecy is invoked to bring time back into phase with place and space, with Earth and Sky, indeed with the particularities of exactly where we are.

Ceremony is a great regulator. When the rites are no longer practiced, then prophecy is told to remind a people of what must be done to restore harmony on Earth. Grandfather David explained, "Each ceremony fits into an annual cycle according to the seasons. All the activities, songs, and dance movements involved in this cycle help keep the Earth in balance, especially the weather conditions necessary for each season." Many Native American prophecies warn that the loss of traditions endangers the environment. Leon Shenandoah, the Tadodaho of the Iroquois, told a group of young Cree, "We always pray for the harmony of the world. If we didn't do our ceremonies in the Longhouse, then this world would come to an end. It's our ceremonies that hold this world together."

There is a close linkage between the wilderness and the lifeways of older nonindustrial cultures and the future of both. One is a lattice for the other. Many elders remember a time when there was respect for wild beings and there was greater harmony on Earth. "Among the flowers I am moving reverently," sing the Seneca. Prophecy is a warning about loss of sacred view, a loss of the reverence that affirms how all creation is related. The stories of the possible future that tribal peoples have told in the past and that are being told now are warnings to us to renew our way of seeing.

Ten years ago, I went to Nahá, the village of Chan K'in Viejo, to meet the *t'o'ohil* (Keeper of the Threshold) of the northern Lacandon. The road to Chan K'in's village was a knotted string of muddy ruts going through endless miles of phantom trees, the few survivors of burning fields and bungled clear-cuts. Every so often, the old-growth forest would appear to remind me of what had been there. I was stricken then to see how deeply the destruction had penetrated into the Lacandon world. It was not sentimentality that informed me but practicality. Destroying these forests was an act of blind stupidity.

It was in these forests that the Lacandon took refuge hundreds of years ago. The end of the world that they knew in the Yucatán was prophesied, and the forests in Chiapas are now falling:

Eat, eat, thou hast bread;
Drink, drink, thou hast water;
On that day, dust possesses the earth,
On that day, a blight is on the face of the earth,
On that day, a cloud rises,
On that day, a mountain rises,
On that day, a strong man seizes the land,
On that day, things fall to ruin,
On that day, the tender leaf is destroyed,
On that day, the dying eyes are closed.
On that day, three signs are on the tree,
On that day, three generations hang there,
On that day, the battle flag is raised,
And they are scattered afar in the forests.

Chan K'in Viejo, when I first saw him in Nahá, was dressed in a wild cotton *xikul,* a rough hand-woven tunic. He was resting in an old hammock with a swarm of children, chickens, and puppies kicking up dust around him. His name, Chan K'in ti' Nahá, means Little Prophet of the Great Water. The eldest son of Bol Kasyaho', he, like his father before him, is the sacred and political leader of the northern Lacandon. I sat on a low stool near the old man as he began to talk about the creation of this world that is now disappearing. No small talk here, just down to the basics of where it began and where it's going. The transformation in the Lacandon world was no big surprise to him. His father told him long ago that their world would be coming to an end, and his grandfather had also told the story. Until recently, the story of the end of the world was projected for a much more distant future.

According to Chan K'in Viejo, the creator of human beings is the god Hachäkyum. He created the Earth as we know it today. The old man told me that the god Akyantho will replace Hachäkyum. He is associated with the north and is the god of foreigners. Akyantho carries a pistol, wears a hat, and dresses in town clothes. Guns, metal tools, money, medicines, foreign diseases, and imported animals, such as cattle, pigs, and horses, are under his influence.

Some Lacandon say that Hachäkyum still dwells some distance from Nahá, in the archaeological site of Yaxchilán on the Usumacinta River that borders Guatemala and Mexico. In the main temple, there is a headless figure. Across from this large torso, resting on the ground, is the figure's head. The Lacandon say that when this head is rejoined to the body, the end of the world will come. They sing to Hachäkyum,

> We are poor and we have suffered.
> This is your ceremony.
> We offer it in your honor.
> We have come to pray to you
> And to weep in your house.
> We have come to speak to you here,
> Here where you live.
> We are poor and could not come before.
> This copal resin is for you.

◣ ◣ ◣

Seventeen years before visiting Nahá, I sat in the hogan of an old Dineh herder named Gray Whiskers. I had traveled by jeep for several days trying to find the place where this old man was grazing his sheep. It had been a fierce winter in New Mexico, and many animals and humans had suffered and died in the ravages of the season. Like Chan K'in Viejo, Gray Whiskers spared me the small talk when I entered his desert home. But unlike the old Lacandon, he held himself in silence for a long time before speaking, before telling the story of beginnings and endings.

He and his wife sat on a pale old sheepskin nestled into the sandy floor of their hogan. A small fire kept us warm in the late winter morning. After an hour of stale coffee and silence, the old shepherd began to talk quietly and slowly. This "telling" was like the southwestern desert, imbued with silence and space. It contrasted with Chan K'in's rain forest quality of fullness and detail. Both accounts, however, were structured to teach the listener about the constancy of change in the body of the great cycles of time. Both men were also clear that it is the human being who affects the quality of the shift from one epoch to another.

And the ending of the current cycle was clearly written in sand and sky, in cloud and star, and in the bodies of the young. In spite of Gray Whiskers's name, he had no gray hair. But, he said, his son did, and so did his grandson. This was one of the signs of this cycle's end, that the young would age prematurely. Another sign was the change in weather. He explained that weather always changes but that the changes heralding the end of generations were characterized by drought and killing storms. His father had told him this, as had his grandfather and his father before that. He also said that the Old Ways were being abandoned. Fewer of the People lived in the way of the season's changes. Few lived a life of prayer and thanksgiving. It seems as if we humans had forgotten, not heard, or not heeded the prophecies of the old ones.

Twenty-five years later, I sat in the yellowing kitchen of a Hopi corn farmer, James Koot-shongsie. For two decades, James had published a newsletter out of Hotevilla, the most traditional of the Hopi villages. *Techqua Ikachi* was a way for a "True Hopi" to communicate to people like us about the Hopi way of life and understanding. With my niece Dana, I arrived on the dark winter eve of *Techqua Ikachi's* final issue and sat into the night with James and Helen, his wife, now nearly blind from diabetes. There we entered into one of those moments when time and culture disappear as James gave the account of the prophecy of his people concerning the shape of the future.

He explained that this Fourth World is nearing its end. All of the signs of the final days are at hand. Not only are we besieged with natural and technological catastrophes, not only were the signs of the prophecy borne out in the predicted two world wars of this century, not only is the terrible "gourd of ashes," the atom bomb, now part of Earth's history, but the Hopi people themselves have lost their balance since the coming of the whites to their mesas. Now there is great suffering—mental, physical, and social—among the Hopi, his people. As the night grew colder and longer, he reminded me that this was the fourth of seven worlds. We had already been through similar cycles on three other occasions. The world was again out of balance, and we were again at the time of purification.

James's small hands were thin, hard, and strong from years of planting corn, beautiful corn, corn so beautiful that seed collectors from all over the world made their way to this humble dwelling on the east edge of Hotevilla. He still worked the Earth, planted and watered his corn, minded his beans and squash, as people have in the Americas for thousands of years. And although his fields were getting bigger, according to James, there weren't so many people planting corn these days in Hopiland. When he lifted his head up toward the naked light bulb to catch a thought, I saw a face that was free of the prophecy. Then his old wild eyes would again capture me in the present as the story unfolded. Balance had been lost, James said. The world was out of harmony. The time of the Fourth World was soon coming to an end.

The next morning, not long out of Flagstaff, as Dana and I drove down Interstate 40 on our way back to California, I saw the dead body of a coyote in the middle of the road. I thought about James and his comings and goings between worlds: his four trips to the United Nations as a spokesperson for the Hopi, his sixteen trips abroad to talk about what the Hopi know. I think that dead coyote made my eyes wet as we drove south because it reminded me of all those old men and women from primal cultures who have recently found a route between the wilds and Western society. I felt grateful to have been born at a time and with a will to be with these old people in their homelands, in the cornfields, in wet forests, in the dust and dark. Would they, like coyote, find their way into the brush of Beverly Hills? I wondered. Or would some of us find ourselves in their world in some other kind of future?

On first hearing the quiet pronouncement of the end of this cycle of life from the old Dineh shepherd Gray Whiskers, I didn't doubt him, nor did I doubt what Chan K'in Viejo and James Kootshongsie told me years later. In 1967, when I met Gray Whiskers, I had already been given a glimpse of the environmental and cultural devastation of the end of our century. As I sensed then and now know, these stories have helped me face the truth of things as they are, even in their changing. They have prepared me in the best way for the worst.

> I live, but I cannot live forever.
> Only the great earth lives forever,
> the great sun is the only living thing.

Prophecy aside, Gray Whiskers, in his late eighties, followed his sheep from grazing ground to grazing ground, as the sun moved through the body of the changing seasons. James Kootshongsie plants his corn and beans. And Chan K'in Viejo, like his Dineh and Hopi counterparts, still enters his *milpa,* where forty or fifty cultigens interact to form a community of plants that supports Lacandon life. Even though these old ones tell us that the end of this cycle is near at hand, even though they are the prophecy tellers, they still plant and herd, talk story and sing. For their knowledge is the knowing of cycles, like the turning of the seasons, the turning of the sky, the turning of the fruitful darkness. They know that the past, present, and future are connected and that the stories support the simple acts of everyday life that can maintain and restore balance and harmony as we travel through the cycle of changes.

In the *Popol Vuh,* the Quiché Maya epic of creation, it is said that the first four human beings had the gift of the gods to see clearly. But the gods were not to make humans their equals and so limited our sight to the obvious—a limitation that can only be overcome with the aid of an *ilbal,* a "seeing instrument," a way to see the invisible world. "This instrument was not a telescope, not a crystal for gazing, but a book, the *Popol Vuh,* or *Council Book.*"

From this book of stories, generations of Mayan Daykeepers understood the nature of cyclical change. The book continues to teach the Maya the cosmic cycles of reality lined out in star and flower bloom. It teaches them about the encounter with death, darkness, and suffering—and about overcoming death. Sun and Morning Star live out their lives as we do, as does the corn, day and night, in an alternating dance of darkness and light.

The Hopi James Kootshongsie told me that winter night that it was too late, that things had gone too far in this cycle. "But we still plant corn in the spring," he said, "and harvest it in the fading light of the early fall. We play with the grandchildren and teach them the Old Ways. We tell the stories of the worlds that we came from and of the world that might emerge." As I left him that night I remembered that according to the Hopi, this is the fourth of seven worlds. Just over halfway in the long body of Earth's time, the Hopi pray:

The day has risen,
Go I to behold the dawn,
Hao! you maidens!
Go behold the dawn!
The white-rising!
The yellow-rising!
It has become light.

Stories and their ceremonies weave our world together: the story of corn maiden and mother, of salmon's death and rebirth, of bear's human wife, of coyote's foul tricks and lynx's loneliness. These stories of ecological conscience are a council where the voices of all species may be heard. It is through these stories that the Earth can be restored, for these eco-narratives are an *ilbal,* a "seeing instrument." Looking through the eyes of others as their ways are told, we may hear and understand the voices of our relatives. Indeed, our mouths can speak a fertile truth. The elders know this; the poets know this:

i speak for the flounder and whale
in their unlighted house,
the seven-cornered sea
for the glaciers
they will have calved too soon,
raven and dove, feathery witnesses,
for all those that dwell in the sky
and the woods, and the lichen in gravel,
for those without paths, for the colorless bog
and the desolate mountains.

In the future, according to some, it is not us who will save the creatures but the creatures who will save us:

> The Crow
> I saw him when he flew down
> To the earth
> He has renewed our life
> He has taken pity on us.

Yes, creation is moving toward us; life is moving toward us all the time. We back away, but it keeps pushing toward us. From radiant space, from luminous darkness, it is approaching us. The elder brothers and sisters see that we have wounded the world, but creation still comes forward. Some of the elder brothers and sisters see that each of us bears the wound that we have suffered upon the Earth. And with this, life cannot help but move toward us. This wound is a door, a gate through which our spirit-hand reaches out to what is moving toward us. Prophecy and story remind us to turn toward creation, toward our extended self. Through the body of imagination, we are reminded of the World Body that gives us life. By destroying this body, we destroy ourselves. By restoring this body, we shall be restored.

The beautiful thing is starting toward me
I being son of the sun
The white-shell bead horse is starting
    toward me
From the center of the sun's home
    it is starting toward me
It eats out of the white-shell basket
The dark clouds' dew streams from it
    as it starts toward me
The pollen from the beautiful flowers
    streams from its mouth
    as it starts toward me
With its beautiful neigh it calls as it starts
    toward me
Soft goods of all sorts are attached to it
    as it starts toward me
Hard goods of all sorts are attached to it
    as it starts toward me
It shall continue to increase without fail
    as it starts toward me
It shall be beautiful in front of it as it starts
    toward me
It shall be beautiful behind it as it starts
    toward me
Good and everlasting one am I
    as it starts toward me.

                                        Dineh

7

The Way of Nonduality

What the people of the city do not realize
is that the roots of all living things are tied
together.

Chan K'in Viejo

Since the mid-fifties, Mexico and the world of her
tribal peoples have been a territory that I could
enter as an initiate, an apprentice to the old ways,
a place near and yet very far from my culture, my
country. From childhood journeys across her
northern deserts, to these recent years when I have
entered the southern Mayan rain forest cultures by
myself and with others, this land of maize with its
history of sorrow and nurture, this wheel of brown
people who hunt and weave, farm and pray, draws
me to it like a lover. Dancing with Huichols in the
stormy Sierra, dreaming with Mazatecs in the
darkness of their Oaxacan nights, drinking *balche*
in the Lacandon wet light of day, I am drawn into
the atmosphere of these experiences whenever and
wherever the copal incense is lit. Over the years, I
continue to return to this world of corn and song,
old gods and brown dust, and worn, dark hands
offering their energies and gifts to the sacred
plants that shape a people's lives.

In the spring of 1990, I went back to the Lacandon village of Nahá to visit Chan K'in Viejo and his family. There was great excitement in the village, not only because the electric line would soon be brought to Nahá, but also because a mahogany canoe was being carved on a nearby mountain. I was not very interested in the pole holes the village men were digging along the road, but the canoe drew me and others up the slippery trail to its carving site. There, two Lacandon men, K'ayum and Antonio, worked with adzes to reduce the canoe's thickness. What a wonderful sight was the moist, peach-colored fresh mahogany.

I had been told by the carver Steve Brown, when we dined together in the highland town of San Cristóbal the week before, that the felling of this huge mahogany tree was an unusual event. It was Steve and his friend Loren White who had brought the adz to Nahá after centuries of ax and machete use by the Mayan peoples. Steve told me that he had never seen such expert carving with ax and machete, and as I was to witness later, the use of the adz had lived secretly inside the Lacandon for all the centuries since the Spanish conquerors had introduced metal tools to the Maya.

Today, there are few mahoganies left standing in these parts. The big old giants and their relatives have been cut down by those seeking arable land or lumber money, leaving the forest torn up and wasted. The people of Nahá have been able to reserve several hundred of the great trees for their use, so when the old canoes rot out or it is time to build a godhouse, a tree is taken.

This particular tree was felled by six men in the old way, Steve told me, but with even more care than usual. Only men whose wives were with child were permitted to cut into the tree. When a giant tree is felled, the jungle heaves; it thunders and roars. Felling a tree is like giving birth. Men with pregnant wives will give proper care and attention to this difficult task, as it is they who will damage least this jungle world in order to protect their wives and their future generations. These trees are alive, say the Lacandon. When a mahogany is transformed into a canoe, it must be fed because it still lives, though in another form. To lose such a living being by cutting it improperly would indeed be unfortunate. So it was that this tree was felled by six men with pregnant wives.

A month later, I arrived with friends to help the men of the village move the canoe from the mountaintop to the lake. This two-thousand-pound vessel was brought down the dark, slippery mountain winched from tree to tree. It made its way through a burned and rocky cornfield, down a long, rugged road, through a marsh, and finally into Lake Nahá. There it would find a new life as the men of the village initiated it through ritual feeding.

Later, we joined Chan K'in Viejo, K'ayum, Antonio, and others in the godhouse for a Balche Ceremony, a ritual done for personal or environmental reasons, including offering thanks to the gods for curing a serious illness or as a firstfruits ceremony. This particular ceremony was to celebrate the completion of the canoe and to offer thanks to the gods for their protection. Without the *balche,* a fermented beverage that bestows ritual purity on those who drink it, Lacandon men and women cannot experience the transcendent state that allows them to communicate with their gods.

Throughout the day, seated on a low stool, Chan K'in Viejo told stories about the gods, as he leaned against a pole in the thatched godhouse. The men clustered around him listened intently. They also enjoyed many laughs as the old man joked about the foolishness of gods and humans. We women were in a small thatched hut on the west side of the godhouse where we had a prime view of the god pots. There we and our Lacandon sisters drank, exchanged gifts, and enjoyed the antics of the men who were feeling the effects of the *balche.*

Late in the afternoon, Antonio carefully offered prayer and *balche* to the gods, who drank it from the god pots, where it is administered in a green rolled leaf of the *xate* plant. We all entered the godhouse and drank *balche* with Chan K'in Viejo, K'ayum, one of the old man's sons, and Antonio. It was then I felt that I was drinking the rain forest's recent human history. As I listened to Antonio and Chan K'in Viejo sing and pray to the gods, I remembered these lines from Bertolt Brecht: "In the dark times / Will there also be singing? / Yes, there will also be singing / about the dark times."

We would drink and drink and continue to listen to the stories told by the old man, and drink some more. The stories were about beginnings and endings, about the revolving of time and the lives of gods and humans. As the day wore on, some of the men passed out, and some had to be carried away by their wives and daughters.

Finally, late in the afternoon, I asked K'ayum when the gods would be fed. He lit the shining resin on top of the god pots, and the fragrant copal was symbolically transformed into tortillas to feed the gods. Then the Lacandon offered their songs of praise, and we offered ours. The black smoke was pouring through the godhouse when K'ayum turned to me and said quietly, "Did you feel the gods arrive?" A short while later, most of us found ourselves lying down on the grass around the godhouse, as if we were all sharing the same dream. For me, it was the forest world dreaming us—the *balche* trees, the mahoganies, the ceibas, the jaguar, the toucan, the cutter ant, the cloud, the rain, the lake.

That night, I thought about the imminent arrival of electricity in the Lacandon village. K'ayum already had a television set. I was at first dismayed with the thought of the social, psychological, and cultural effects that might come with it. I was afraid for the Lacandon. But later I realized that their lifeway cannot be preserved as a cultural specimen. They are embedded in the same net of relationships that we are. Their rain forest home produces oxygen, weather, petroleum, and hardwoods that fuel or build the technological society north of them. Their community is also unfolding in response to their relationship with our world. The village owns a truck; it has an airstrip

131

and now electricity. One of the temptations to be avoided is the impulse to "preserve the past." The little airstrip and road to Nahá have already ended such a possibility if it ever existed.

After leaving Nahá, I saw that the Lacandon world is certainly not antiquarian. The Lacandon of Nahá are fortunate to have such a man as Chan K'in Viejo in their midst. Not married till he was fifty, he was being prepared to help his people through this time of radical change and uncertainty. His sons, Chan K'in Presidente and K'ayum, an artist, and his grandson Mario are being prepared by him to carry on the traditions of their people. I once asked K'ayum, whose paintings have been exhibited in Mexico City, the United States, and Spain, why he continued to live in Nahá. He grinned widely as he replied, "Why would I want to live elsewhere? I have been to our capital, to your country, and to Spain. There is no better place to be than here. The climate is sweet. The forest is beautiful. For generations my people have lived here. I am part of this world. The forest is my home, my family. I understand everything here. I am content here."

I asked that same question years ago of Don José. He, like K'ayum, loved the environment in which he lived. He was interested in our world, but the truth of his life lived in the forest and deer, the peyote and corn, and in the body of fire, Grandfather Fire, the first shaman. All these were his relatives and part of the ancestral continuity that supported his life and his people. Always adaptable, he traveled to many parts of the world in later years, but he returned to his homeland with a certain relief. There everything was so much more beautiful, so much more alive. And there the sacred mountains, caves, and springs still were homes to the Ancestors.

When Don José sat in front of a fire in his village, he saw Tatewarí, our Grandfather Fire, the oldest god among the Huichols and the special deity of shamans. Directly or through the magical deer Kauyumari, also known as Our Elder Brother, Don José would reveal the wishes of the gods through his dreams and visions. Grandfather Fire is mediator between gods and humans and the one who led the first Huichols in the peyote hunt, the actual and legendary ground where Huichol myths are generated. He is, as well, the protector of human beings, giving the *mara'akáme,* the shaman, the power to heal.

Ramón Medina Silva explained to the anthropologist Barbara Myerhoff why Tatewarí is so precious to his people. Fire is their Grandfather. When Fire is brought out of wood at the beginning of a ceremony, the people weep because "Grandfather is arriving," and when Grandfather is with them, all the worlds are reconciled in this relationship of intimacy:

> Why do we adore the one who is not of this
> world, whom we call Tatewarí, the one who
> is the Fire? We love him because we believe
> in him in this form. Tai, that is fire, only fire,
> flames, Tatewarí that is the Fire. That is the
> mara'akáme from ancient times, the one who

warms us, who burns the brush, who cooks
our food, who hunted the deer, the peyote,
that one who is with Kauyumari. We believe
in him. Without him, where would we get
warmth? How would we cook? All would
be cold. To keep warm our Sun Father would
have to come close to the earth. . . . That
is why we adore him, why we have him
in the center, that one who is Our Grandfather.

In the mid-seventies when Don José, whom
we called Abuelo or Grandfather, flew to New
York City, the pilots of the plane were convinced
that he was Carlos Castaneda's Don Juan. Having
never been outside of Huichol territory, the old
man had dressed in his finest ceremonial garb to
celebrate his journey. He had on his shaman's
wide-brimmed straw hat with hawk feathers flut-
tering at the crown. He wore white deerskin san-
dals and brightly embroidered pants and shirt.
When he arrived in New York, we settled into the
basement of a brownstone on Waverly Place.

One day, he pointed out to me that the sun had
not shined in New York's stony canyons for the
two weeks he had been there. He often laughed at
brownstone living and made great jokes about
"these North American cave dwellers." But mostly
he was disturbed that we did not understand the
relationship between ceremony and Our Father
Sun. He said that the Sun Father depends on the
offering of human joy for his light to shine. Our
Father the Sun loves to see the people happy,

singing and dancing. Without this, he becomes sad and will withdraw his light from the world. Thus it was in New York.

Don José remarked that the people of these northern cities had forgotten to celebrate their lives and in this way had lost their connection to Father Sun and also to Our Mother the Sea, who brings the rains. We had forgotten that we are related to Sun and Sea. We had ceased to appreciate the life that had been given to us. The old shaman would try to reawaken in us this sense of wonder, this love for Earth and Sky, for our Mother and Father, Our Grandmother and Grandfather, our sacred Brothers and Sisters, but would we be receptive? Here was a man who had never seen a bathroom or a fireplace with a chimney. But when we went to see the film *2001*, he already knew the strange world entered by the space hero from his experiences with dreaming and with peyote.

Though we might interpret Don José's perception of our alienation from the beings of Earth and Sky as metaphor, for him it was neither a psychological nor cultural reflection but direct experience. He really saw us as cave dwellers living our lives in dreamless darkness, separated from the ground of life—our relations. He was often incredulous that we were so out of touch with reality, the reality in which everything is kin.

Years ago, this old corn farmer presided at a rain ceremony in Big Sur, California. There had been three years of drought in California, and he insisted that we were making the wrong offerings to Tatéi Haramara, Our Mother the Ocean. "If she is your Mother," he said, "why do you throw garbage into her?"

Before the ceremony, he looked at us sternly, then laughed as he explained that there was to be a battle between him and us, his assistants. He had the power of Kieri Tewíyari, the datura sorcerer, and would throw datura pollen into our eyes and blind us (as if we weren't already quite blind). In this way he would effortlessly prevail. The ceremony went through the night with many people crying and dancing, praying and singing. It was a beautiful and terrible night. I sat at the old man's feet for twelve hours watching my friends struggle and weep against the wall of life. One and then another turned their backs away from the altar and cried unashamedly. What in life had they betrayed? Whom had they forgotten or abandoned? Where had their joy gone?

Just before dawn, the net of suffering seemed to break, and the chanting and drumming carried the sound of laughter. At first light, Don José touched me on the shoulder and pointed his deformed hand toward the window. Rain was falling for the first time in three years. Rain would continue to fall for days, and swollen with rain, the mountains would fall. They would fall like offerings to the ocean.

Later that morning, we walked down to the shore of the gray and churning Pacific and made the usual offerings to Tatéi Haramara, Our Mother the Ocean. Standing on the cold, rocky shore, we left small bits of chocolate, green parrot feathers, and lighted candles. Laughing, the old man told us that it was not so difficult to provide the right atmosphere for rain. You just have to know how to treat your relatives.

We go into the darkness, we seek initiation, in order to know directly how the roots of all beings are tied together: how we are related to all things, how this relationship expresses itself in terms of interdependence, and finally how all phenomena abide within one another. Yes, the roots of all living things are tied together. Deep in the ground of being, they tangle and embrace. This understanding is expressed in the term *nonduality*. If we look deeply, we find that we do not have a separate self-identity, a self that does not include sun and wind, earth and water, creatures and plants, and one another. We cannot exist without the presence and support of the interconnecting circles of creation—the geosphere, the biosphere, the hydrosphere, the atmosphere, and the sphere of our sun. All are related to us; we depend on each of these spheres for our very existence.

> All is a circle within me,
> I am ten thousand winters old.
> I am as young as a newborn flower.
> I am a buffalo in its grave.
> I am a tree in bloom.
> All is a circle within me.
> I have seen the world through an eagle's eyes
> I have seen it from a gopher's hole.

I have seen the world on fire
And the sky without a moon.
All is a circle within me.
I have gone into the earth and out again.
I have gone to the edge of the sky.
Now all is at peace within me,
Now all has a place to come home.

Originally, I understood interconnectedness in terms of the Buddhist notion of *pratityasamutpada,* or conditioned co-arising, which says that everything that occurs is conditioned by and conditions everything else. As my meditation practice continued and I spent more time in the wilderness, I began to feel that all creation shares a common skin. This sensibility inspired me to look at the ways that our common flesh is experienced by tribal peoples and Buddhists.

I have for years felt strongly that it is important for us to discover directly this ground of reality, this web of mutuality. The experience of interconnectedness, however one might come to discover it, changes how we perceive the world, and thereby all our relations with the phenomenal world become an expression of an extended self, a self with no boundaries.

As I suggested in the chapter on language, each category of being appears to have a language of its own, be it the stars in their celestial motion or the fragrant grasses in their smell and their seeding. Zen Master Dogen said not all beings speak with a human tongue:

You should entreat trees and rocks
to preach the Dharma, and you
should ask rice fields and gardens
for the truth. Ask pillars for the
Dharma and learn from hedges
and walls. Long ago the great god
Indra honored a wild fox as his
own master and sought the Dharma from him,
 calling him
"Great Bodhisattva."

All the different forms of language are a means by which we give substance to our connection with one another. Through language and story, we weave ourselves into the world. It isn't so much that language and story confirm the ground of reality, but rather that they constitute the ground itself. According to the Dineh, language creates the world and all of its interconnections. All beings through their relationship with others hold a story at each node of connection. These stories inform creation. They carry the continuity that flows through all relationships and are about the Great Sangha, the whole community of Earth.

In Buddhism, the term *sangha* refers to the community that practices the Way together. I ask, Where is the boundary of this community? From the perspective of elder cultures, *sangha* does not necessarily stop at the threshold of our next of kin or even our own species. Community for many peoples includes plant and animal, features of the landscape, and, of course, unseen ancestors and spirits.

For many tribal cultures, Earth has long been seen as a whole and living organism. It has been intimately described as mother, father, friend, lover, and extended family. Earth and its life forms and systems, including mountain and river, salmon and cedar, is experienced by most tribal peoples as alive and sentient. It is a great Being whom we can talk to and hear from, and with whom we can exchange energies. The Inuit Richard Nerysoo puts it this way: "Being an Indian means being able to understand and live with this world in a very special way. It means living with the land, with the animals, with the birds and fish as though they were your sisters and brothers. It means saying the land is an old friend and an old friend your father knew, your people have always known. . . . To the Indian people our land is really our life."

The frontier of community, extending beyond the human being, includes the sacred mountains that surround our homeland, the rocks and springs that have given birth to civilizing ancestors. The eagle, bear, buffalo, and whale—wisdom beings of Sky and Earth—are allies and teachers. Crow, raven, coyote, and jay are the local clowns. Community can be lived in and experienced as a whole system of interrelated forms and species engaged in common activity. And from a Buddhist perspective, this community is alive, all of it, and practices the Way together.

Because I spent the winter sleeping with a fish, there is a fin within me now.

Because I spent the spring with an eagle in her
  nest,
there is an egg within me now.
Because I spent the summer with the buffalo,
there is a bone within me now.
Because I spent the autumn growing with one
  tall tree,
there is a root within me now.

The biologist Lynn Margulis says that life is a social event. It is composed of communities and collectives, from communities of microorganisms to communities of creatures and plants. These communities and collectives find themselves within other communities, and nested within them are other living communities as well. Earth is a being of many families, of many clans, interacting in an unceasing exchange of energy, an ongoing exchange of information. Earth is as well a vast event of communication. Chang-tsai, an official in eleventh-century China, expressed this experience of relatedness in these words, which he placed on the west wall of his office:

Heaven is my father
and earth is my mother
and even such a small creature as I
finds an intimate place in its midst.
That which extends throughout the universe,
I regard as my body
and that which directs the universe,
I regard as my nature.
All people are my brothers and sisters
and all things are my companions.

For some tribal peoples, the creatures that they eat and the plant life that is used for medicines, foods, and other commodities are relatives that are respected. Sadie Marsh, a Wintu woman, recalled that her grandfather would rise early each morning, wash his face, and then pray to Olelbes, the One Above, the creator of the world. He would then talk intimately to all that was around him—the rocks and trees, the salmon and sugar-pine:

Oh Olelbes, look down on me.
I wash my face in water, for you,
Seeking to remain in health.
I am advancing in old age;
I am not capable of anything more.
You whose nature it is to be eaten [deer],
You dwell high in the west, on the mountains,
high in the east, high in the north, high in the
    south;
You, salmon, you go about in the water.
yet I cannot kill you and bring you home.
Neither can I go east down the slope to fetch
    you, salmon.
When a man is so advanced in age, he is not in
    full vigor.
If you are rock, look at me; I am advancing in
    old age.
If you are tree, look at me; I am advancing in
    old age.
If you are water, look at me; I am advancing in
    old age.
Acorns, I can never climb up to you again.
You, water, I can never dip you up

and fetch you home again.
My legs are advancing in weakness.
Sugar-pine, you sit there; I can never climb
   you.
In my northward arm, in my southward arm,
   I am advancing in weakness.
You who are wood, you wood,
I cannot carry you home on my shoulder.
For I am falling back into my cradle.
This is what my ancestors told me yesterday,
they who have gone, long ago.
May my children fare likewise!

When the Dineh used to hunt deer, they would strip the slain deer of its flesh and respectfully lay its bones and horns on boughs from north to south. If the first deer killed was a buck, a turquoise bead would be placed between its horns. Then a prayer was recited: "In the future that we may continue / to hold each other with the turquoise hand." The hand that killed and skinned the deer is turquoise, something precious and rare. It is a hand of respect. The deer's life is taken, confirms the hunter. And the deer returns as dawn and jet, yellow dusk and zigzag lightning, haze, flowers and beautiful vegetation. In these forms, the deer returns. This same sense of respect was shown to the salmon, according to my friends of the Northwest Coast. Their elders offered salmon bones to the river that their salmon relatives could be reborn.

And what about vegetation, the trees and plants, are these too our relations? In the early

1900s a Fox Indian from Mississippi explained this relationship of respect for the life of the trees in the following way: "We do not like to harm the trees. Whenever we can, we always make an offering of tobacco to the trees before we cut them down. We never waste the wood, but use all that we cut down. If we did not think of their feelings, and did not offer them tobacco before cutting them down, all the other trees in the forest would weep, and that would make our hearts sad, too."

This respect for trees is well understood among the Warao, who live in the Orinoco delta of Venezuela along the Caribbean seaboard. *Wa* means "canoe," and *arao* means "people": the People of the Canoe. According to the anthropologist Johannes Wilbert, the Warao believe that the forest is a tribe of animated bushes, palms, and trees. Some of them were given origin by old gods, others are metamorphosing, and still others have always been "tree people." The red cachicamo tree, used for canoes, is thought of as the Mother of the Forest, known as Dauarani. She is the guardian of the forest, and in earlier times, she prohibited the killing of large mammals and the unauthorized felling of palms and trees.

The trees and palms, to the Warao, are like other people with whom they have kinship ties and trade relations. When a Warao man wants to become a master canoe maker, he must first receive an invitation from Dauarani, the Mother of the Forest. If he is granted permission to create a new canoe, he is in effect sacrificing one of the daughters of Dauarani. Before he cuts down one of her daughters, both Dauarani and the victim, her daughter, must consent to the act.

If permission is given, the canoe maker–initiate and a shaman-intercessor approach the tree-maiden, who appears in the shape of a young woman with a comb in her hair and a necklace of blue, white, and red beads. Before the work crew arrives, the shaman-intercessor sings to her: "Don't become upset. Be happy and smile at me. I am like your own offshoot. I am the one you accepted. I am fond of you. I came to touch your body, to caress you lovingly."

The maiden smiles and replies. "You are a neo-phyte master canoe builder. I can tell from your new ornaments. Do with me according to your vision: Kill me and thrust me down on the very soil that raised me." The tree-maiden and shaman-intercessor continue this dialogue until the work crew draws near. She then enters the tree that is to be sacrificed.

The shape of the canoe, when completed, is like a vagina, and each time the man enters his canoe, he enters the daughter of the Mother of the Forest. The canoe is also the vagina of the Mother of the Forest, and the bounty or cargo that issues from her womb supports the canoe maker's family and his community.

Women of the Warao are not shamans or canoe makers. They are professional herbalists who have a developed relationship with the "tree people" of the forest. Johannes Wilbert's son, Werner Wilbert, spent much of his childhood with the Warao. He learned the traditions of the

Warao women when he was a child in their midst. He reports that the women trade with the "tree people" for medicines, food, and various commodities and, like the shamans and canoe makers, attempt to live in a relationship of mutuality and interdependence with the forest.

This sense of mutuality with the natural world is confirmed among the Lakota of the North American plains through their seven rites, including the ceremony of the Pipe (Chanunpa), the Sun Dance (Wiwanyag Wachipi), and the vision quest (Hanbleceya). The Inipi Ceremony or the Sweat Lodge existed before the coming of the Pipe to the Lakota people and is used to purify those who participate in it of that which separates them from their relatives, including their nonhuman kin.

Twenty years ago I entered the Sweat Lodge for the first time. Ten years later, I was adopted by the Lakotas Grace Spotted Eagle and Wallace Black Elk. They were to build a traditional lodge deep in the canyon in Ojai where I lived during the 1980s. I remember the concern I felt about the possibility that we would lose control of the fire that was heating the rocks. There had been no rain that summer, and the land was dry as dust. Grandfather asked me if I wanted him to pray for rain, and of course, I responded in the affirmative. It rained so hard that we could barely keep our first fire alive.

In the tradition of the Lakota, the words you say when you enter the Lodge, *Mitakuye Oyas'in*, mean "All my relations." You pray that the experience of purification is not just for the betterment of the individual but for the sake of all beings. Another perspective of this prayer was put forth by Frances Harwood, who suggested to me that it means "I *am* all my relations." The more beings that I affirm I am related to, the more extensive my being: I take shape in the bodies of all my relations, and the boundary of my soul increases infinitely when I see that I am related to all of creation.

Entering the darkness of the Stone People Lodge, crawling on one's knees through the low door into the womb of the lodge, being cleansed by the four elements of Earth, Water, Air, and Fire renew the experience of relatedness. Grandfather Wallace told me years ago, "We go into that sacred lodge to purify ourselves. We go in there to see just who we really are, and in that darkness to see how we go on this Earth. We make ourselves really humble, like the littlest creature, and we pray to Spirit that we may be healed, that all may be healed. We see that we are not separate from anything. We are all in this together. And we always say 'All my relations' to remind us why we are doing this."

The Lakota also confirm their relationship to all beings through the Chanunpa, the sacred pipe. The pipe is made of wood and stone and often adorned with feathers of the spotted eagle, the creature who flies highest, sees farthest, and represents Wakan Tanka. In it, red willow bark, *chanshasa,* is smoked. When held by human hands and offered, fire and breath unite in prayer and join the realms of Earth—mineral, plant, creature, and human—to the sky and Spirit.

Long ago, I was taught that the Chanunpa was introduced to the people by White Buffalo Spirit Woman. She showed the Lakota that praying with this portable altar was and continues to be a way for the people to remember their greater family. As the late Lakota elder John Fire Lame Deer told the story, when White Buffalo Spirit Woman presented the Chanunpa to the People, she explained to them, "With this holy pipe, you will walk like a living prayer, your feet resting upon the grandmother, the pipe stem reaching all the way up into the sky to the grandfather, your body linking the Sacred Beneath with the Sacred Above. Wakan Tanka smiles on us, because now we are as one, earth, sky, all living things, and the *ikce wicasa*— the human beings. Now we are one big family. This pipe binds us together."

▲　▲　▲

The wisdom of the peoples of elder cultures can make an important contribution to the postmodern world, one that we must begin to accept as the crisis of self, society, and the environment deepens. This wisdom cannot be told, but it is to be found by each of us in the direct experience of silence, stillness, solitude, simplicity, ceremony, and vision.

The deep ecologists Arne Naess, Joanna Macy, and John Seed write about the ecological self, the experience of our interconnectedness with all of creation. They know as well as I do that these words are intellectual concepts until this self is directly experienced. This is understood in Buddhism, where experience or "direct practice realization" is contrasted with conceptual knowledge. Buddhism as well as tribal traditions emphasize direct learning. In the tribal world, and I dare say in ours, Truth is not easily made real in our everyday lives, nor is it easily described.

Among Native American peoples, one must purify oneself, empty oneself, sacrifice one's self for it. Sweat baths, emetics, fasting, silence, prayer, solitude, and other practices make one ready for Spirit. Entering the Stone People Lodge, you get on your knees, make yourself humble and crawl into the darkness. Going on the vision fast, you leave food, water, and the world behind. If you are a Pima from the Southwestern desert, you make a pilgrimage to the end of the world to gather salt and then step over this edge into the ocean.

And what do you see? In the Lakota elder Black Elk's account of the Hanbleceya, the rite of the vision fast practiced by his people, the prayer made by the elder wicasa wakan on behalf of the "lamenter" speaks not only to the young man who was going out on the mountain to cry for a vision but also to remind us of why we go to wilderness places: "All the Powers of the world," said Black Elk, "the heavens and the star peoples, and the red and blue sacred days; all things that move in the universe, in the rivers, the brooks, the springs, all waters, all trees that stand, all the grasses of our Grandmother, all the sacred peoples of the universe: Listen! A sacred relationship with you all will be asked by this young man, that his generations to come will increase and live in a holy manner."

In the beginning my people were one people.
They were made of feathers and corn.
They were made of dust and bone.
My people rode the tail of the sun
And swung on a rope through the sky,
My people lived inside the earth
On water running backwards into time.

One of the ways we can characterize what Black Elk called "a sacred relationship" is by the term *nonduality*. What I mean by nonduality is that we are intimately connected; in fact, we are intimate. We abide in each other. Nonduality may well be a perception and experience that is revealed only to the innocent. Many of us, no matter the skin color, no matter the culture or epoch, have found that we have to leave society to retrieve our innocence. Our minds and bodies need to be refreshed; they need to be restored to each moment. Gurdjieff once said that the only way you can get out of jail is to know that you are in it. Jail here is not our daily lives but our alienated relationship to the world of the familiar. We must retrieve the magic of the ordinary and rediscover sacredness in each thing.

Black Elk did not keep his vision to himself. It

was not his personal and private enlightenment. He had seen the fabric of Spirit's cloth, and he knew that all things are woven of this same stuff. He told his friend John Neihardt: "While I stood there I saw more than I can tell and I understood more than I saw; for I was seeing in a sacred manner the shapes of all things in the spirit, and the shape of all shapes as they must live together like one being."

When I sit with old Chato, a Cora who lives alone in the mountains of Baja California, I listen to him talk about the Juarez Mountains and sense that he is describing himself, the part that is innocent and not self-conscious. He has climbed up these rocky ridges and down these rugged canyons until they are in his stride, in his voice. Walking behind Jorge K'in in the rain forests of Chiapas, my self-centeredness recedes as I fall into his complete familiarity with this dark, wet terrain. Following Ogobara across the cliff tops of Dogon country in central Africa, I know that the strength of these cliffs and the openness of the desert below are no different from this joyful old man. In no time we are somehow walking in the same feet as we make our way across the body of his life.

In our bones is the rock itself;
in our blood is the river.

This wisdom of a common flesh, a common heart, is expressed in the Papago rain song collected by Ruth Underhill:

151

At the edge of the mountain
A cloud hangs.
And there my heart, my heart, my heart,
Hangs with it.

At the edge of the mountain
The cloud trembles.
And there my heart, my heart, my heart,
Trembles with it.

According to Paul Shepard, "Ecological thinking . . . requires a kind of vision across boundaries. The epidermis of the skin is ecologically
like a pond surface or a forest soil, not a shell so
much as delicate interpenetration. It reveals the
self ennobled and extended . . . as part of the
landscape and the ecosystem, because the beauty
and complexity of nature are continuous with
ourselves . . . we must affirm that the world is a
being, a part of our own body."

Our skin is a membrane that connects us with
the world around us, just as the space between
you and me actually connects us as well. But we
have protected "our skin" and "our space" at the
expense of our own lives. We are discovering that
we are already in what the phenomenologist
Maurice Merleau-Ponty has called the "Collective
Flesh," the world itself as an intelligent body.
Earth now is revealed as a vast being who is the
ground of our perceiving, dreaming, and thinking.

We share the same body and the same self.
Ch'an-sha, a ninth-century Chinese Zen monk,
said, "The entire universe is your complete body."

Shunryu Suzuki Roshi said, "Tathagata is the body of the whole earth." Walt Whitman wrote, "I am large. . . . I contain multitudes." And Thich Nhat Hanh says in the Zen *gatha* he composed to be recited before eating,

> In this plate of food,
> I see the entire universe
> supporting my existence.

It was in the mid-eighties that I went to France to meet the Vietnamese Buddhist teacher Thich Nhat Hanh, a poet and human rights activist. Plum Village, his home in the Dordogne, is found in an old landscape of archaic initiatory caves and hills covered with sunflowers, plum trees, and grape, redolent of the great fertility of the Earth. Here in the quiet hills Vietnamese and Westerners gather each summer to practice meditation and deepen their sense of rootedness in the dharma. Many of the people who come here have lost their homeland, or their sense of home.

Thich Nhat Hanh's expression of the teachings of the Buddha is very relevant to our understanding of the relationship between the natural world and culture. He coined the word *interbeing* as a translation of the Vietnamese phrase *tiep hien*. This is the name of the Buddhist order that he founded in 1964 during the war that destroyed the peoples and forests of his homeland. The word *tiep* means "to be in touch with" and "to continue." *Hien* means "to realize" and "to make it here and now."

According to this perspective, to be in touch with the inner reality of mind and to understand the reality of the outside world is to discover that they are woven into one fabric. In our everyday lives, inner and outer appear to be separate and distinct. But when looking deeply, we find that there are no separate realities. All apparently distinct phenomena are folded into one deep continuum. This is called, in Buddhism, nonduality, or the unity of self and other.

The word *continue* or *tiep* points to the view in Buddhism that there is no birth or death, no beginning and no end. Yet in our everyday world, all phenomena are constantly changing. The very nature of physical existence involves interaction and transformation.

One day during meditation practice at the Ojai Foundation, as I was following my breath, I suddenly experienced my body breathing. I was not breathing; my body was breathing. I knew in that moment that my body will return to Earth one day, and I asked myself if that meant that I would cease to exist. It was clear then that my seeming separate identity as a body will cease to exist, but I will continue in an unceasing wave of causes and effects. In that moment, I had entered the mindstream beneath the waves of causality.

Two weeks before, I had delivered my mother's eulogy in North Carolina. Her body was ashes now, but she lived on through her friends, relatives, and good works in the world. "To continue" means that one's original nature is not altered or destroyed by the changes of state through which one passes.

The word *hien* means "to realize," to make life real, to enter fully the present moment. The medieval alchemists used the image of a man putting his head into the mouth of a lion to symbolize the potency of the realization of the present moment. The sun with its brilliant light is another symbol that points to the burning presence of reality. I know that by entering the body of reality we will see our world in its joy and suffering at this very moment. Only if we do this can we respond with understanding, compassion, and enlightened activity, knowing that we are not separate from any being. That which is real does not exist in the past. Nor does it exist in the future. The present moment in its completeness is the only true time-space for the experience of reality.

When the Lakota say, "All my relations," they are weaving themselves into the fabric of reality. Yet most of us tend to identify ourselves with the relative world of the particular and not also with the vast context of which we are one expression. Buddhists often use the image of the wave and the water to explain this idea. If we are a wave, it might be difficult for us to see that we are also water. A wave can arise in response to Earth's movement or the sun's heating the atmosphere and awakening wind. Water's response to the elements allows for a separate identity to emerge. But we often get locked into our smaller identity—that which comprises the particular—and we lose the simultaneous perception that we are both wave and water, both human and nature.

When we begin to have a sense of the fabricated nature of who we are in the social or relative sense, we commonly experience a crisis. We often create another social role to make ourselves feel secure. We put on another hat, find another job, change religions or relationships.

Yet we have a deeper identity as well. This "other identity," beyond our psychosocial one, is both about relationship and process, and also empty of any distinctions and free of boundaries or qualities of separateness. It is like the water that is cloud and rain, stream and ocean. Thich Nhat Hanh uses the image of the droplet of water that finds itself in a cloud. In response to its increasing weight as other droplets join it, it falls to Earth as rain, loses its identity as a cloud and raindrop, and becomes part of the stream in the valley below. One day, the stream's identity as stream might lose itself to the great ocean. But one thing never changes: water is always water. Even as identities change through time, its true nature as water persists.

The Japanese Zen Master Hakuun Yasutani Roshi used to say that the fundamental delusion afflicting humanity is to suppose that I am here and you are there—that is, duality. If I want to understand the interconnectedness of phenomena, it means that I must realize nonduality in my life in a practical way. Mahatma Gandhi's experience of interbeing was expressed by living with the economically impoverished. He transformed

"I" and "them" into "we," believing in the essential unity of all human beings and, for that matter, of all that lives. Gandhi tried to reach self-realization through selfless action; in other words, through the realization of nonduality in the experience of identifying with those who were suffering and the activity of nonduality that he called nonviolence.

The Western dualistic perspective regarding mind and nature or self and other suggests that there is a world outside us, and then we have our inner world, a world of feelings, perceptions, and mental formations of various kinds. Many of us think that our mind is separate from the world around us. Gregory Bateson said that this divided notion of the self was the great epistemological error of Western civilization. He made the point that the individual mind is immanent not only in the body but also in the pathways and messages outside the body. There is a larger mind of which the individual mind is only a subsystem. This mind is immanent in the totally interconnected social system and in our planetary ecology.

> Soil for legs
> Axe for hands
> Flower for eyes
> Bird for ears
> Mushroom for nose
> Smile for mouth
> Songs for lungs
> Sweat for skin
> Wind for mind

The Buddhist experience and practice of non-duality arises from a perspective that says there can be no consciousness without an object. To be conscious means to be conscious of something. Looking deeply in meditation practice, we discover that we are both subject and object, whether we are suffering "out there" or "in here." From this perspective, helping to free other beings is to free a part of one's self. Our personal wounds and the World Wound are not separate.

Years ago at a small gathering of friends and thinkers, Gregory Bateson asked Jonas Salk where mind was and then quickly pointed his finger to the space between the two of them. We can ask the same question of ourselves about the nature of the self. Where is it, our self? If you are from the West, you would tend to point toward yourself. If you are a villager in Mexico, you might point toward your immediate community. If you are a certain kind of Buddhist, you might say that the self does not exist. If you are another kind of Buddhist or a deep ecologist, you might say that the self is coextensive with everything else.

Deep ecology and Buddhism teach us that if we penetrate with real awareness our own minds then we also can understand that we are not separate from the world around us. World and mind, mind and nature, self and other, our breath and the atmosphere are not separate from each other.

I entered the life of the brown forest
And the great life of the ancient peaks, the
    patience of stone, I felt the changes in the
    veins

In the throat of the mountain, . . . and, I was
   the stream
Draining the mountain wood; and I the stag
   drinking; and I was the stars,
Boiling with light, wandering alone, each one
   the lord of his own summit; and I was the
   darkness
Outside the stars, I included them, they were a
   part of me. I was mankind also, a moving
   lichen
On the cheek of the round stone . . . they have
   not made words for it, to go behind things,
   beyond hours and ages,
And be all things in all time, in their returns
   and passages, in the motionless and timeless
   center,
In the white of the fire . . . how can I express
   the excellence I have found, that has no
   color but clearness;
No honey but ecstasy; neither wrought nor
   remembered; no undertone nor silver
   second murmur
That rings in love's voice.

The physicist Erwin Schrödinger explored
whether consciousness should be considered singular or plural. From the outside, he noted, on
the explicit level, there seemed to be many minds,
but looking deeply he saw that there was only one
mind, that consciousness was singular. Years ago
in Ojai, I heard the physicist David Bohm describe this as an implicate order in which everything is linked to everything else in the universe,

and in which one discovers the whole universe implied in each thing, in every particle.

In the current popular Western worldview, that which is not us is outside who we are and is therefore "other." The view held in physics and new biology and, as I have mentioned, in deep ecology as well as Buddhism is that there is a self that is coextensive with all phenomena—what has been called by the deep ecologists the ecological self.

Thich Nhat Hanh has suggested that this view of nonduality can be called nonviolence or "awareness." Awareness shows us who we really are, of what we are composed, and what we are actually doing at this very moment. "A human being is an animal," writes Nhat Hanh, "a part of nature. But we single ourselves out from the rest of nature. We classify other animals and living beings as nature, acting as if we ourselves are not part of it. Then we pose the question, 'How should we deal with Nature?'" He recommends, "We should deal with nature the way we should deal with ourselves! We should not harm ourselves; we should not harm nature. Harming nature is harming ourselves, and vice versa. If we knew how to deal with our self and with our fellow human beings, we would know how to deal with nature. Human beings and nature are inseparable. Therefore, by not caring properly for any one of these, we harm them all."

We are in and of nature from our very beginning. Human society and our relationships with one another are important, but our selves are richer in the continuum of interconnections, not only with other humans and the human community as a whole but also with creatures, plants, and the bioregion that we inhabit. And now, with the changes to the atmosphere bringing drought and storm, we are beginning to see that our lives and the weather are coextensive with each other, interpenetrate each other, and are interdependent. Indeed, we humans are not separate from "our atmosphere."

I'm in it everywhere
what a miracle trees lakes clouds even dust

We can ask, Does a rock have sentience and beingness? A sea? A desert flower? "Inanimate objects, do you have a soul?" (Lamartine). From our perspective, rock, sea, and flower not only "are" but also share beingness in an undeniable pattern of relationships. A thing cannot "be" in isolation; rather, the condition of beingness implies interconnectedness, interdependence, and interpenetration. From this perspective, one seemingly separate being cannot be without all other beings and is therefore not a separate self but part of a greater Self that is alive and has reflexive awareness within its larger Self. An eighth-century Chinese monk asked, "It is said that insentient beings, inanimate objects expound the Dharma. Why do I not hear it?" The disciple of the Sixth Ancestor of Zen Nanyang Huichung answered, "Although you do not hear it, do not hinder that which hears it."

We are Nature, long have we been absent, but
   now we return,
We become plants, trunks, foliage, roots, bark,
We are bedded in the ground, we are rocks,
We are oaks, we grow in the openings side by
   side,
We browse, we are two among the wild herds,
   spontaneous as any,
We are two fishes swimming in the sea to-
   gether,
We are what locust blossoms are, we drop
   scent around lanes mornings and evenings
We are also the coarse smut of beasts, vegeta-
   bles, minerals.

Many poets and Zen masters realize that we
are all things, all beings, that we interpenetrate
one another and are coextensive with all creation.
We inter-are. This point about beingness, relatedness, and interpenetration can be illustrated with
the simple example of maize, the corn that we
cultivate, pray with, or eat. For many native farmers of the Americas, this ear of corn is a living
being, even a mother. Her cob is covered with
kernels of life that give forth generations. She cannot grow to maturity outside of the body of Earth,
so therefore she is part of the Earth. Nor can she
grow without sun, moisture, and human care.
Embedded in her very nature is earth, sun, wind,
rain, and human being. She also nourishes the
people who tend her. Without her nourishment, if
you are a Hopi or a Maya, for example, there is
not the physical energy to cultivate her. She is a

staff of life, something on which many depend. She also is connected to and dependent on all that which sustains her.

Maize is offered not only to hungry bellies but also to the gods and ancestors because she is a nourisher of all life, past, present, and future. She is called beautiful by many because all aspects of her feed life. Her fertilizing pollen is used to heal. Her outer sheath, her husk, is used to hold sacred tobacco that is smoked in ceremony. Her stalk is burned in the springtime, and its ashes restore the Earth. She cannot "be" in isolation. Rather, she is part of the continuum of life whose unique expression of maize-ness is part of an interactive web of identities and events that give rise to her beingness. She is sun and rain, night and day, earth and wind, human and ancestor.

The Tewa say that the first mothers were corn, and it is they that give the souls to the children. In this way, they pray to the Corn Mothers:

> Our old women gods, we ask you!
> Our old women gods, we ask you!
> Then give us long life together,
> May we live until our frosted hair
> is white; may we live till then
> This life that now we know!

The Lacandon and other Mayan peoples say that they are corn. They are what they eat. The Arikara, who were farmers and hunters of the plains, said that Corn Mother descended into the Underworld and brought the human race into this world. The description of the human's journey from the Underworld is like the corn plant's gestation and maturation.

As I am writing this, I am in the Juarez Mountains of northern Baja California. In the field down the hill from me, the old Cora Chato is slowly harvesting his corn. Stony mountains are all around us. These mountains form a rugged landscape of pale granite boulders woven with piñon and sage. Several days ago I sat on a boulder outside the cabin and gazed toward Cañon de Guadalupe. I realized that my mind and that which I was perceiving were not separate. My mind had not left me to journey to tree, crow, cloud, and boulder. These things were one with me. They had penetrated me, been absorbed by me, were inside me; or I was absorbed by them. The distinction between inside and outside had disappeared. Separating ourselves from that which appears outside us is like trying to separate color and light, waves and water, our breath and the atmosphere.

There are infinite expressions of this experience of interconnectedness and interpenetration, of nonduality. Thich Nhat Hanh uses the example of the sun that exists "out there" in the sky but also exists within us as warmth, as energy. We take the transformed energy of the sun as food into our bodies, and it becomes not only energy but flesh, bone, and blood. We depend completely on the sun for our lives, and the sun lives within us. The sun is our bodies, and we are an expression of the sun's body. We then actually share one body, the sun's true body.

These notions of interbeing, interrelatedness, interdependence, and interpenetration are not far from the ideas of bootstrap physicists who see that not even particles can exist independently. No phenomenon can exist just in and of itself. There is no essential self, no separate self. Sitting in this high desert in Baja, I can see that the tree does not exist independent of the atmosphere. The sage blossom is not separate from the summer storm. The crow is not separate from the coyote.

When I feel within my bones the truth of the interconnected nature of all creation, I know that we have greatly underestimated our true identity. We feel that our self is confined to our ego, to the sense of "I-ness" that stops with our skin. Carlos Castaneda has called this self-centered, anthropocentric view "self-importance," a kind of human chauvinism at the expense of everything else. Chakdud Tulku Rinpoche, a Nyingma teacher, calls this "self-cherishing." This coercive and exclusive view is part of our cultural baggage. It was definitely part of my childhood, raised as I was on the Book of Genesis, the story of our origins.

As a child, I thought that the description of a world where creatures were in dread of us was adult nonsense. Now, there is a kind of strange, ironic, and tragic truth in this familiar passage found in Genesis: "And the fear of you and the dread of you shall be upon every beast of the earth, and upon every fowl of the air, and upon all that moveth on the earth, and upon all the fishes of the sea; into your hands they are delivered."

The fear and dread experienced by the creatures has penetrated into our relationships with one another and even with ourselves. Our alienation attacks our bodies, and against ourselves we have no defense. In what seems to be an existential crisis of planetary proportions, our very existence is threatened as we destroy ourselves through the destruction of the Earth. Our alienation is expressed in split atoms, schizoid psyches, and divided selves, human against human, nation against nation, and human against nature. This view that expresses itself in how we describe the world—of subject doing something to object—is a profound error of perception, a delusion of the self.

True self-interest therefore includes more than ourselves. Our lives depend completely on the retrieval of the sense of the deep continuum, the stream of our being, known through our connection to the ancestors, the continuum of creation that is our history, and the continuum of mind and nature, of self and other that is immanent everywhere. This continuum flows from the secret room hidden in the core of our bones. It is retrieved in the darkness where the roots of creation tangle and feed.

Knowing how deeply our lives intertwine
  We vow not to kill.
Knowing how deeply our lives intertwine,
  We vow to not take what is not given.
Knowing how deeply our lives intertwine,
  We vow to not engage in abusive relation-
  ships.
Knowing how deeply our lives intertwine,
  We vow to not speak falsely or deceptively.
Knowing how deeply our lives intertwine,
  We vow to not harm self or others through
  poisonous thought or substance.
Knowing how deeply our lives intertwine,
  We vow to not dwell on past errors.
Knowing how deeply our lives intertwine,
  We vow to not speak of self separate from
  others.
Knowing how deeply our lives intertwine,
  We vow to not possess any thing or form
  of life selfishly.
Knowing how deeply our lives intertwine,
  We vow to not harbor ill will toward any
  plant, animal, or human being.
Knowing how deeply our lives intertwine,
  We vow to not abuse the great truth of the
  Three Treasures.

                              Stephanie Kaza

8

The Way of Protectors

Oh my little brother,
Don't you know that I sing your song?
I sing to the markings of your coat.
Do you hear how I sing to your ears?
How beautifully marked is your tail.
You come along the trail,
Oh my little brother.
As you come you tear up the earth.
Don't you know that I sing your song,
Oh my little brother?

Chan K'in Viejo

In the late 1980s, I was in the Lacandon rain forest with Jorge K'in, an older man of the Jatate Lacandon. Jorge lives in the village of Lacanjá, the main settlement of the Southern Lacandon near the well-known ruins of Bonampak and Yaxchilán. One day, some friends and I went for a day's walk with Jorge and members of his family to the unexcavated ruins of Lacanjá. The small trail took us through thick green forest wet with recent rain and alongside rushing, brown swollen rivers.

During our walk in the *selva,* Jorge seemed to disappear with each step as he moved along the trail. At one point, however, he stopped in his tracks and said in a rough voice, *"Culebre! Muy peligroso!"* (Snake! Very dangerous!).

There is only one thing I have not wanted to encounter in the rain forest of Chiapas. That is the famed *nauyaca,* the four-nosed viper. I had heard many stories from my Yucatec friends about this aggressive snake, how it chases its victims down the trail, leaping after them. Needless to say, Jorge and all of us had come upon a *nauyaca.*

The old man expertly herded the snake off the path and then ordered me to have my friends move on past him. This was accomplished with some difficulty because the dozen of us were spread out down the trail at great distances from one another. I watched Jorge with utter fascination as he held the viper with his gaze. He did not move, nor did the serpent. It took fifteen minutes for the group to make its way past this strange scene. Waiting nearby, I heard a rifle shot. Jorge had killed the snake.

Later I asked him why he had killed it. He paused to change cultures and languages, from Lacandon to Spanish, before he replied that children frequently traveled this way. I definitely had mixed feelings about the snake's death. There was no question that I was relieved, but I also felt more than a nagging sense of regret. In my younger years, I had had many close encounters with rattlesnakes, and we seemed to have found a way to coexist. Like the poison oak that grows abundantly in the Sespe Wilderness near Ojai, poisonous snakes engender respect and mindfulness.

"Poisonous" plants and creatures can be invoked as protectors, protectors of place. Within a bioregion, they protect the deeper forest and are allies to their ecologies. As allies of human beings, they protect against drowsiness and insensitivity, preventing us from charging through fragile terrain with a heavy foot and blind eye. They teach alertness and respect as we interact with place. They also evoke certain qualities within humans. One can like the jaguar stalk and enjoy the night, blend with the environment and disappear into its body. Protectors teach humans to sing like wolf, to go inside like bear, and to relax like snake.

Human beings have for a long time destroyed the protectors of the wild regions. For many humans, these plants and creatures are dangerous and mean suffering or death. They represent something evil in the world, on this Earth, that should not be ignored. They excite the impulse to eradicate, to kill. Their power both fascinates and intimidates. Here is the enemy! And wolf and mountain lion are shot; coyote is poisoned. That which requires one to be more careful, more mindful, is eliminated. And with the passing of wolf and rattler, poison oak and thorn, passes the integrity of the habitats they guard.

> The temple of the animals has fallen into
>   disrepair.
> The pad of feet has faded.

Those who encounter creatures must subdue the noisy and dispersive aspects of their minds and bodies so as to be in harmony with these beings, or enter into conflict with them. In the wilder regions of this planet, I have encountered allies and protectors in various shapes and sizes. Even my studio on the ridge in Ojai was a dwelling for a snake who drank from the water bowl next to my outdoor sink. We must not continue to systematically eliminate the very elements and presences on Earth that protect and instruct us.

In the early eighties, the artist Robert Ott took me climbing up to the watershed high above the West Fork of the Sespe River. He had found a pristine waterfall cascading in front of three grottoes, below which was a tiny emerald pool into which the clear water fell. This pool held the reflection of a wild tiger lily on its surface. There was no sign that human beings had ever been there, and both of us felt a kind of presence that was abiding in this cool, wet, green corner of the dry, rugged wilderness. We offered a prayer arrow to the driest of the grottoes, spent the night, and in the morning, vowed to return the following year.

The next spring, we and some others made our way down the trail to Tar Creek and the Sespe River in the Los Padres Wilderness north of Ojai. I had never seen so many rattlesnakes out and about. Some were the ordinary brown color; others were coal black. One lay dead alongside the trail: five feet long, the rattles removed, blood oozing from a bullet hole, its big, old lifeless body was a sad storyline about the loss of what is strong in these parts, including condor and mountain lion.

Later that day, one of our party was pursued by an old grandfather rattler who was saying in no uncertain terms, "Watch your step!"

We made our camp on the sandy bank of the Sespe River in the early evening. Falling asleep in no time, I was abruptly awakened by terrified screams. One of our party had been visited by yet another rattler. Exhausted, once more I fell into a dreamless sleep, to be awakened at eleven the next morning by Robert, who told me that he had visited the waterfall at dawn. Coming out of my sleep, I asked him if he had seen any rattlers. He replied, "Yes, I was bitten by one." And indeed, as I looked with astonishment and concern at his wrist, there was a small fang puncture and the black-and-yellow marks and swelling of a hemotoxic reaction.

Robert, wanting to find the source of the waterfall, had had a clear intuition that he was to go no farther than the grottoes. He proceeded nonetheless. As he climbed above the fall, he put his hand on a rock where it turned out a small rattler was resting. As the snake bit him, he jerked his arm over his head, and the snake flew toward the tumbling water. He then sat down "to absorb the situation." He realized that he had gone too far. He knew better but had let his curiosity get the best of him. He saw the snake as his ally teaching him respect not only for this place but also for his intuition. He also saw the snake as a protector of this high, wet corner of wilderness.

Later that day, we walked toward a wide place in the river to swim. We were to encounter no more snakes during our time in the West Fork. Needless to say, we took little for granted those next days along the river. At night the frogs, crickets, and owls were our companions, and on our last day the condor appeared.

◢ ◢ ◢

In Zen meditation practice, you face the wall and hope that in this process of yielding, you face yourself and realize who and what you really are. The basic impulse in Mahayana Buddhism is proclaimed in the vow to save all beings. The translation of the vow of the bodhisattva that I first heard years ago referred to all "sentient" beings: people and perhaps animals. But lately I have chosen to drop the word *sentient* from the vow when I share it with others. I no longer think that this distinction is relevant. Saving a cedar tree is as important as saving the life of a wolf or the patch of poison oak that shelters the wood rat's nest. Wood rat, cedar, wolf, and poison oak all have a right to live, and we and they are interconnected in ways that are only now being understood.

I also now know that awareness and sentience, including intending, are expressed in many ways in the life of the planet. From the ecological, Buddhist, and shamanic perspective, sentience is part of the greater picture of the living universe. I have looked out of the eyes of rocks and mountains, and although I know that the psyche yearns to give the world a soul, I am not totally convinced that there is not in fact a kind of awareness in the mineral and plant world. In any case, I don't forget the advice given by Nan Yang Huichung when he said that we should not hinder any being who hears deeply. When I drop into the stream of existence in a finely tuned way in the course of practice or ritual process, I discover how excluding is the worldview of the West, and I do not want to hinder that which hears the subtler voices of Earth.

There is a difference in a life that is lived on the level of the universal or general and one that is lived through the experience of detail and with the sense of the particular strongly present. The Buddhist teacher Richard Baker Roshi encourages his students to examine in detail the social and physical environment. We need to do this in order to acknowledge fully and completely our biological and physical world and how our social institutions and personal views shape our lives and our planet. Industrial cultures have rejected the biological, the earthly. It is not always neat and manageable, predictable and controllable. In excluding the biological, they have transformed allies into enemies.

When we exclude the wilder elements of our nature, culture and society become our focus. The idea of "humankind" has had a profound and beneficial impact on the shaping of democracy in the West and has created the ground for the development of "human rights" and a more compassionate response to human suffering. As Baker Roshi has pointed out, this notion of "humankind" is in part coercive in that it often excludes those other than humans from the development of a greater identity that is not limited to self and our own species.

I am sure that the vow of the bodhisattva does not exclude those who are not human. It is also clear that our identity is not limited to what is wrapped up in our own skins. This means that the human being is not the only being with rights, or its form of thusness. This is a revolutionary notion for the West: not only that the cedar and the whale have a right to live in a decent habitat but also that their absence from the net of existence could leave us impoverished, unguarded and exposed.

I often use the symbol of the mandala or medicine wheel to illustrate the notion of interconnectedness and nonexclusivity. A mandala from the Buddhist perspective is a complete system emerging from the field of emptiness. It is a map as well as a protector. Within the mandala are elements that have given rise to a pattern of existence, and as such it can be a symbol of the individual as the world or the universe. The mandala, or medicine wheel, is seen first of all as a womb with the potential for all forms of existence within it. It has a center, and that center represents the midpoint of the self. But the self is not exclusive of all else that is included within the body of the mandala. The mandala also has within its body four directions of life, four ways of being that represent balance in the world, interrelatedness, completeness, and movement.

In this form, we might find represented the world of plants in the south, the world of minerals in the west, the world of creatures in the north, and the world of humans in the east. The four directions could also represent the four elements—Water, Earth, Air, and Fire—and the four qualities of our life as human beings—the world of feelings, the emotions; the world of form, the body; the world of cognition, the mind; and the world of spirit. At the center is consciousness. Interfusing all these elements is emptiness.

When we contemplate such an object of meditation, we discover that if we remove any element from the design, the whole picture collapses. We also discover that all the elements are interconnected and thus dependent on one another. None can exist, from this picture's perspective, without the presence and activity of all of the others.

The medicine wheel or mandala can be used in meditation practice and ceremony as an object of contemplation that teaches us about the relationship between the relative world of changing forms and the Absolute of its background of emptiness. If used as a meditation or ritual device, it can also teach us that existence is more adhesive, extensive, and inclusive than we have previously understood. It can as well be a map for use in meditation or ritual that indicates a territory to be entered and explored.

Meditation and ritual have opened for peoples in many cultures the roads between human beings and unnamed and unexplored worlds. The gateways to these realms are guarded by Protectors who test our resolve, our keenness of mind and heart, our friendliness toward the unknown. We meet these Protectors in those personal experiences and collective rites that are Threshold experiences, where the husk of alienation is broken down.

The word *threshold* means "the place where things are thrashed or beaten apart." It is one place where we make immediate the present. In such a place we discover that we are immersed in each other; we are mixed up with all beings. Only because of differences can beings be linked together in relationships; distinctions imply relationships. Relationships call us into the body of initiation.

The shaman's experience of initiation is one of the best examples of how the Threshold works to reverse the process of suffering and misfortune into its opposite, to transform an adversary into a Protector. The pattern of initiation in many cultures follows the same course. The shaman can be abducted by or seek out a predatory creature who takes him or her to the Underworld. In the Lower Depths, the shaman encounters all manner of terrifying spirits and creatures and in many cases is dismembered and consumed by them. He or she has yielded to the forces of destruction and death and in so doing has lost the ground of culture, history, and psyche.

Free from the confines of society, shamans can enter into communion with the very beings who have attacked and ravaged them. The beings that abducted and annihilated the shaman then become teachers for the neophyte, and he or she can embody the qualities that they exemplify. Losing the battle, the shaman becomes all-victorious. This process is a kind of transmission between species. Those who were the shaman's enemies become Allies and Protectors. Often this process is a kind of psychological homeopathy. The shaman is overwhelmed by an enemy or poison, and through the process of surrender to these forces, the power that overtook the shaman becomes his or her strength. Thus enemies are transformed into allies. Poison is transformed into nectar. Obstacles become gateways.

Both Buddhism and shamanism are based in the psychological grammar that says we cannot eliminate the so-called negative forces of afflictive emotions. The only way to work with them is to encounter them directly, enter their world, and transform them. They then become manifestations of wisdom. Our weaknesses become our strengths, the source of our compassion for others and the basis of our awakened nature. Thus, according to Buddhist psychology, anger can be transformed into mirrorlike wisdom or clarity; pride can be transformed into equalizing wisdom or equanimity and generosity; desire can be transformed into discriminating wisdom or discernment; jealousy can be transformed into unhindered wisdom or enlightened activity; and ignorance can be transformed into the wisdom of our True Nature, or clear and energetic intelligence.

This is a radical perspective for Westerners to consider because so much of our culture is based in the denial of negative emotions or in the psychology of removing afflictions instead of transforming them. But as we deny these afflictive realms of the psyche, they are projected into our bodies as disease, into other individuals, groups, cultures, and nations, or out into the more untamed parts of nature. In our contracted state, we set out to destroy that which is actually the source of strength and energy of our greater identity.

▲   ▲   ▲

One winter I sat with Jorge K'in and friends in his banana patch and turkey yard in Lacanjá with the bright moon overhead. I was remembering our first meeting, when friends and I had sung songs for him and his family as a way of bridging the cultural and language gap. This produced a response of song from him, sung in secret, far from the ears of the people of his village. I had heard these songs twenty-five years before at Columbia University, when I worked on the project that analyzed song and dance style across cultures. The project's director, Alan Lomax, had returned from the Soviet Union in 1964 with an enormous folk music collection. I spent years in the archives at Columbia listening to the songs of cultures that no longer existed.

The most striking music for me was the animal transformation songs of Siberia. The long phrases, broken occasionally with glottal shakes, ended with the breath and were followed by a gasp. These songs seemed to hold stories and evoke landscapes that were too wild to pause for evenly spaced phrases. I had not heard these songs since but longed to, for they seemed to be a treasure of the Paleolithic continuity that still existed somewhere on the planet.

That first night in Jorge K'in's hut in Lacanjá brought tears to my eyes. For twenty-five years I had searched for these songs. That night in his smoky hut, I heard the songs of a hunting culture that had survived time and vast geography. His songs were about animal transformations, not the Siberian bear or tiger but the jaguar. The songs seemed to resonate with some deep part of my past as well. He could not sing them within earshot of his neighbors as most of them had left the traditional ways and converted to Christianity. But the old man sang them to us whenever he could, as often as he could. They seemed to liberate him into himself, a truer part of himself that walked in the *selva* like a free man.

Jorge, my friends, and I were to walk together again in the *selva*. On this visit, Jorge K'in's rifle was broken, and I felt a mixture of relief and concern, remembering the *nauyaca* he had shot. But this year, our ally would take a different form. That is the Way of the rain forest. The path, though the same, is always changing.

This time on our way to the Lacanjá ruins, there were many signs of jaguar. All along the small trail on which we were walking were places where a jaguar had "rasked" to sharpen her claws. The deeper we went into the *selva*, the more frequently these signs appeared. The clawed earth and root affected me in a number of ways. I was relieved that jaguars still roamed in these forests. The human population of this area grows each year with families seeking land to cultivate. This, combined with the increase in logging and cattle ranching, the presence of Pemex, the Mexican national oil company, and the refugees from war-torn lands south of Chiapas has made deep inroads into the *selva*.

Judging from the size of the claw marks, this was no small cat. With each sign, I became much more alert, much more awake, again realizing that without a rifle, we were not at the top of the food chain. The signs of her presence were very, very fresh. She obviously was just ahead of us and knew what we were and where we were. We continued to follow her trail with quiet steps.

In an hour or so, we found ourselves on top of an unexcavated temple of old Lacanjá. Resting there in the damp late morning, Jorge sang one of the old songs of his people. After he had finished and we had rested a while in the silence of the *selva,* I asked him to tell us what the song was about. It was a long and complex story about a woman changing into a jaguar and a jaguar changing into a woman. As I recall, she was a hazard to be reckoned with.

We then made our way down the rubble of this old temple that was crowned with a huge mahogany and began to walk through pure rain forest off the trail altogether. Jorge wanted to show us a special ruin with unique circular columns. And we walked and walked, up wet ravines and down steep, leafy, slippery hills. We continued to walk into the afternoon. It seemed as though we were lost.

After a while Jorge and his son, Chan K'ayum, left our small group of friends on the side of a hill and ranged about looking for a trail or familiar sign. We sat there for a long time, at first enjoying ourselves and then wondering if the *duendes,* the local "little people" renowned for befuddling forest travelers who do not make proper offerings, had not created a bit of a problem for us. It was clear that no one in our party could have gotten us out of there before nightfall.

I wondered if the jaguar was looking on this scene with some amusement. I certainly was. Just the week before, we had been in the bowels of the Temple of Inscriptions in Palenque, and the lights were extinguished as we sat quietly on the steps next to the sarcophagus of Pakal. It was a long, dark walk up to the temple's crown to discover that our quiet and the hour had indicated to the caretaker that no one was down there at closing time. So here we were again, near closing time.

At last, Jorge and Chan K'ayum showed up, and we all felt somewhat rescued and more than a little relieved. We made our way to other old and forgotten temples and fallen stelae green with moss. We then swam in a big bend in the river before making our way home. All the while, the jaguar's signs preceded us.

Shortly before we left the forest, I smelled something unbelievably strong. It was such a jolting odor that my stomach turned and my hair stood on end. Twenty feet later, I came upon a good gallon of freshly deposited cat scat studded with big, lead-colored flies. I cracked up. If I had had a hat on, I would have taken it off. What an ally, this beast, this wild meat-eater. What an ally. That night we celebrated Passover in Jorge's turkey yard. Instead of lamb shank, we ate mango.

▲ ▲ ▲

Every existence is poison to some and
    spirit-sweetness to others.
Be the friend. Then you can eat from a
    poison jar and taste only clear
    discrimination.

Rumi

9

The Way of the Ancestors

We shall live again
We shall live again
Comanche

In Plum Village, after one of Thich Nhat Hanh's dharma talks in Vietnamese, he invited people to put photos of their deceased relatives in a book placed on the altar. Practicing Buddhism is about discovering ourselves to be in a great flowing river of continuities. Just as our mothers, fathers, and grandparents live inside of us, so do generations upon generations of mothers and fathers before them. Part of our task is to discover how all our ancestors continue to inform our lives, and the same holds true for all forms of life. For we have been shaped not only by our human ancestors but also by the environments in which they lived.

Plum Village, in the old, rich, and fertile Dordogne, feels like very familiar ground to me. I remember coming to this part of southern France as a child in the mid-fifties. I felt right at home then in this place that has been inhabited for tens of thousands of years. Paleolithic peoples used its caves as shrines in which to worship and dream awake the hunt in their depths. Neolithic peoples

farmed its rich land. And today, orchards, vine-
yards, and great fields of sunflowers flow across
these old hills. As I sit in meditation each day on a
bright ridge overlooking this history, I feel the
ancestors of the Dordogne making themselves
known to me. I also feel the land itself, the wind
and light rain of summer, and the oaks and
berries, as well as the brown viper hiding in the
thorns. These beings in their generations have
been around for a while too. My senses tell me
that I am part of this continuity here in southern
France. I have stepped into a river that includes
history, and that river also lives inside of me.

It was in Plum Village that I began to question
our relationship to the dead. I wondered if we can
see beyond personal histories of loss and grief to
an autobiography that includes the loss of forests
and rivers. I wondered if we can look at what has
passed from life on this Earth and see how the absence of so many species touches us at this very
moment. Have so many species of creature and
plant passed into extinction that the sense of the
particular is now lost? I wondered if somehow we
can redeem these dead and prevent the ending of
blue sky and bright wind.

Aldo Leopold, the father of wildlife conservation, wrote about a change of heart, a change of
understanding that he went through on seeing a
dying wolf that he had shot:

> We reached the old wolf in time to watch a
> fierce green fire dying in her eyes. I realized
> then, and have known ever since, that there

was something new to me in those eyes—
something known only to her and to the
mountain. I was young then, and full of trig-
ger-itch; I thought that fewer wolves meant
more deer, that no wolves would mean
hunter's paradise. But after seeing the green
fire die, I sensed that neither the wolf nor the
mountain agreed with such a view.

This story recalls the words of the poet Theodore Roethke in his "Journey to the Interior": "But
when I breathe with the birds / The spirit of wrath
becomes the spirit of blessing, / And the dead
begin from their dark to sing in my sleep." Those
species that are now extinct cannot be made whole
again. Those that we know about might live in the
conscious part of our memories. The anonymous
ones, those that have passed from this Earth without the human mind being aware of them, are
spectral forms even in our deepest memory. But I
am sure that they too sing in our sleep.

I know that sense of not knowing a life form.
However, the one I am thinking about now as I
write this is still with us. One spring, I visited the
Monterey Aquarium in California, where my attention was caught by a film about plankton. I had
seen still photos of these minute bodies of living
pattern, but observing them in motion stopped
my breath. I had no "idea" that there could be so
many strong but tiny expressions of life, each one
so distinct and beautiful. Plankton continues to
live in the oceans, but many other species are
being lost for eternity every day. I know that we

cannot redeem that which is forever lost; this is sure. But it is not impossible to consider that the myriad ancestral forms of life are indeed worthy of veneration.

Tribal peoples often venerate their dead. Sometimes it is to appease the spirit's sorrow or anger at being separated from the world of the living. At other times, the dead are honored for the protection that they offer or the gifts they bestow. The dead can be venerated out of love and respect for what they have given to the living, in life or through their deaths. By venerating the dead we can experience the fullness of our own souls. Losing touch with these ancestors, we lose touch with the soul, both theirs and ours.

I believe that the psychic retrieval of the souls of the dead is about our own soul retrieval. It is about soul-making. Earth can only be redeemed if we reach through the veil of this loss to touch what is now forever gone. The redemption of the dead, the veneration of the ancestors of all life forms, returns us to a river of life that flows from the past into the present moment to nourish Earth and the future.

◣　◣　◣

In Chaco Canyon, New Mexico, dwellings that were inhabited by a vital culture a thousand years ago are now abandoned and crumbling. In this part of the world, the Pueblo people know that the ancestors, when not forgotten, are changed into clouds that nourish Earth with rain.

As I write this, in southern France, there is no water flowing out of the taps. There has been drought here for several years, and now in the ceaseless white heat of summer the water supply is low. When I was in New Mexico a month before, open fires were not permitted because of drought conditions. I try to remember that according to the Pueblo peoples of the Southwest, when we venerate the ancestors, the rains fall. When we forget the ancestors, the rains cease.

We are connected to the dead of every kind in ways not commonly remembered. The bones of the ancestors, which lie in the body of Earth, are transformed into the bodies of plants and creatures, including us. The Dineh who live in and around Chaco Canyon understand that they are an intimate part of this ancestral continuity as expressed through mountains, mists, clouds, and generating rain. They know in their bodies, in their bones, that they are directly connected to the mountains that gather the cloud, the green that gives rise to clouds, and the mist and ultimately the rain that nourishes all that grows to give forth the beautiful pollen that fertilizes and heals. In all these forms, the ancestral continuity confirms our true identity.

> The mountain, I become part of it.
> The herbs, the fir tree
> I become part of it.
> The morning mists, the cloud, the gathering
>   waters,
> I become part of it.

The sun that sweeps across the earth,
I become part of it.
The wilderness, the dew drops, the pollen,
I become part of it.

By feeding on the ancestral remains of countless plant and animal species, the great trees of tropical and temperate forests literally translate the past into our atmosphere. The destruction of these old forests is an attack on one of the most vital ways that the ancestors express themselves to Earth—as our very atmosphere. I don't wonder that Southwestern peoples know that when the ancestors are forgotten, the rains cease to fall. It is ironic that the great transformation we are currently wreaking on our atmosphere involves the use of animal and vegetable fossils in the form of petroleum and its by-products. We have missed the point; a different sort of transformation is required.

This thought was brought home to me when I sat in the kitchen of the Hopi farmer James Kootshongsie one cold December night. At the time President Bush and Saddam Hussein stood a world apart with a war pending between them. In the quiet of this humble scene, James looked at me and said, "Listen, my friend. We have forgotten where we have come from. We have forgotten the worlds before this one. We have returned to a time of chaos, and life is hanging in the balance. Can you hear this, daughter? Do you understand what I am saying?"

▲   ▲   ▲

In old Earth cultures, the shaman is the servant of the people, the gods and ancestors, the creatures, plants, and elements. When the world is out of balance, the shaman redresses this disequilibrium. In these cultures, illness is understood as a loss of the sense of connectedness, of relatedness, of continuity—the experience of a kind of existential alienation. This alienation expresses itself as a divided self, a self that has forgotten the extensiveness of its being.

Like Tatewarí of the Huichols, the shaman has the duty to help restore balance by opening and renewing the lines of communication between realms. This involves sacrificing or giving up inflated and corrupt civilization and returning to a simpler, more fundamental existence. It also means the restoration of traditional and ceremonial life that honors the continuum of creation. In essence, the veneration of the ancestors confirms the continuity of existence in time and space or place. The world is brought back into balance through the renewal of ceremonial life that confirms that continuity.

We think that the ancestors are behind us, but they are actually those who go before us. They are a vanguard, a spirit wave that pulls us along. When the Hopi enter the kiva, they go into the body of the past to ensure the future. We too must seek initiation and search the darkness of the past for the light that is hidden by time. For thousands of years, initiation has served to establish the individual firmly in the continuum of all existence. To see ourselves as part of the continuous body of interconnecting, interdepending, and interpenetrating members—past, present, and future—is one of the functions of Buddhist meditation practice. And until we give birth to our ancestors, Earth cannot be redeemed from its suffering. To exclude any species from the continuum of existence—either consciously or unconsciously—is to deny part of ourselves.

Those who are dead are never gone:
They are there in the thickening shadow.
The dead are not under the earth:
they are in the tree that rustles,
they are in the wood that groans,
they are in the water that sleeps,
they are in the hut, they are in the crowd,
the dead are not dead.
Those who are dead are never gone,
they are in the breast of the woman,
they are in the child who is wailing
and in the firebrand that flames.
The dead are not under the earth:
they are in the fire that is dying,
they are in the grasses that weep,
they are in the whimpering rocks
they are in the forest, they are in the house,
the dead are not dead.

Birago Diop

10

The Way of Compassion

May my body
be a prayerstick
for the world.

Many Buddhists have believed that Bodhisattva Avalokiteshvara is beyond gender. According to the *Lotus Sutra,* this deity transforms the body and becomes a female, male, soldier, monk, god, or animal to save various beings from suffering. When he/she looked out into the world and saw the immense suffering of all beings, he/she shed tears of compassion. One of these tears was transformed into the Noble Mother Tara, the embodiment of wisdom and compassion in Tibet. Tara traveled across China and to southeast Asia and Japan. She syncretized with local protectresses, old Earth and Water Goddesses, who combined with the wisdom being Tara to give birth to Kuanyin (China), Kuan Seum (Korea), and Kanzeon (Japan), "Listening to the Sound of the World."

In her display as Avalokiteshvara, she has six heads with which to perceive the world in all its forms and a thousand arms and hands to help those who are suffering. She has given herself to the world to be shaped by its needs. All her hands hold instruments of effective action. Like the Mother of the World, she is outside us, but like our own mother, she lives inside each of us as well. In fact, she lives inside each thing. She can be found everywhere—in the falling rain that nourishes the Earth and eases the summer's heat, and in the starving child who awakens our compassion. She is the part of us that enters the body of communion without hesitation. She enters this body naturally and fearlessly.

This kind of responsiveness is pointed to in the Eighty-ninth Case of *The Blue Cliff Records* when Yunyan asks Daowu, "How does the Bodhisattva Kanzeon use all those many hands and eyes?" Daowu replies, "It is like someone adjusting their pillow at night." In the dark, reaching with feeling, beyond conception and the rational mind, here compassion is a natural response to the world, not mediated by thought or rule or law or vow or intent, not regulated by religion or social duty. "The compassion of the undifferentiated body of no-cause comes burning forth," says Yasutani Roshi. And Daowu says, "Throughout the body is hands and eyes." This is the mystery and pervasiveness that we can know only in our hearts. Like our blood, it penetrates us completely.

The eyes of Kanzeon see into every corner of Calcutta. The ears of Kanzeon hear all the voices of suffering, whether understandable to the human ear, or the voices of felled cedar and mahogany or struggling sturgeon who no longer make their way up Mother Volga to spawn. The hands of Kanzeon reach out in their many shapes, sizes, and colors to help all forms of beings. They reach out from the ground of understanding and love. "Let the beauty we love be what we do. There are hundreds of ways to kneel and kiss the ground" (Rumi). It is understood that the craft of loving-kindness is the everyday face of wisdom and the ordinary hand of compassion. This wisdom face, this hand of mercy, is never realized alone but always with and through others. The Buddhist perspective shows us that there is no personal enlightenment, that awakening occurs in the activity of loving relationship.

Gandhi was once asked by a friend if his reason for living in a village and serving the people there was purely humanitarian. Gandhi responded, "I am here to serve no one else but myself, to find my own self-realization through the service to these village folks." Gandhi's reply implies that there is no separation between self and other. India's liberation is Gandhi's liberation. He is not separate from a villager any more than you and I are separate from the very atmosphere that we breathe.

This natural generosity is practiced in many forms in elder cultures. Spiritual practice among Lakota peoples is grounded in the expression "All my relations," which proclaims that spiritual activity is not only for those immediately participating in it but for all beings everywhere. Antonio Garcia of the San Juan Pueblo explains how the spirit of generosity is at the heart of his religion. "When I was a kid I remember everything we did was religious. My parents used to get up in the morning, they'd take sacred cornmeal, they'd blow their breath on it so the gods would know who they were and they'd feed the gods and they'd ask for good weather, they'd ask for rain, and they'd ask for good fortune for everybody, not only people of the Pueblo, but everybody in the world. Now that is beautiful."

Sometimes the medicine person does this through the practice of extreme empathy. Flora Jones, a Wintu shaman from Northern California, heals through the experience of "feeling with" the patient: "I feel for the sores, the aches, and the pains. When I put my hand over the body I can feel every little muscle and every little vein. I can feel the soreness. It hurts me. If they have heart trouble, my heart just beats. Any place they are hurting I hurt. I become a part of their body." The Japanese Zen poet Basho Matsuo says it this way: "Unless we see or hear phenomena or things from within the things themselves, we shall never succeed in recording them in our hearts."

In Buddhism, the metaphor of Indra's Net from the *Avatamsaka Sutra* has been used over the generations to exemplify how not one thing is separate from any other thing even though things are different from each other. At each intersection in Indra's Net, there is a shining and distinct jewel. Sustaining the light from all the other jewels, each jewel reflects all the jewels in the Net and has no real or separate self nature. A single jewel and all other jewels thus exist in a pattern of presence and mutual activity.

If we consider this metaphor in terms of our own lives, we can see ourselves as both qualitatively different from and at the same time made of the same stuff as the rest of the planet: different but equal. From one perspective we are part of this Net; from another perspective, we are the whole of the Net of Jewels itself, with its myriad of forms reflected in our existence. Here there can be no domination of self over other or other over self. Instead, all beings, including each one of us, enemy and friend alike, exist in patterns of mutuality, interconnectedness, and co-responsibility and, ultimately, in nonduality.

Buddhism, shamanism, and deep ecology are ways for us to understand and realize that this Earth is a vast and rich network of mutual arisings, dyings, and renewings. Seeing this, we experience ourselves as part of the world around us, and the world around us is part of us. It is from this base that authentic harmlessness and helpfulness awaken.

Arne Naess makes the point that we need environmental ethics, but if we feel we are being unselfish, if we believe we are giving up, even sacrificing, our true interest in order to show love for nature, this is probably in the long run a treacherous basis for conservation. Through a genuine experience of identifying with all beings, we may come to see our own interest served by conservation, through genuine self-love, love of a widened and deepened self, an ecological self.

When we plant a tree, we are planting ourselves. Releasing dolphins back to the wild, we are ourselves returning home. Composting left-overs, we are being reborn as irises and apples. We can "think like a mountain," in Aldo Leopold's words, and we can discover ourselves to be everywhere and in everything, and we can know the activity of the world as not separate from who we are but rather of what we are. The practice of the "nonlocal self" means that when we work for the restoration of the rain forest, we are restoring our "extended self."

Leaving behind the anthropocentric view that holds us away from the world and discovering how we are related to and indeed embedded in all that exists has profound political and environmental implications. The Earth is imperiled. It is suffering. Living as part of its body, we suffer with and through it. Awakening through this suffering, we might be able to help the Earth and ourselves, heal it, and thus heal ourselves. The Zen monk Dogen wrote, "You should know that the entire earth is not our temporary appearance, but our genuine human body." Earth, according to Dogen, is truth and speaks truth but not always or necessarily with a human tongue. It is our body. And its voice can be heard even in the desert silence.

We can ask ourselves, then, When will we see our True Eye? When will we discover our True Hand? Kanzeon has innumerable hands. They appear in every shape and color. She is everywhere, hearing the suffering of Earth. Kanzeon is Earth, as well, in its many forms of suffering and beauty. Her hands reach out through clear-cut forests, poisoned rivers, and hungry children to awaken us.

Her hands reach back to herself through our compassionate response to victims of war, slaughtered rhinos, and grasslands that are now wastelands.

Once Richard Baker Roshi asked if I thought the birds would sing more if they knew we were listening. It seems as if we are clearly being asked to listen to the sounds of the world. The migrating birds that used to pass through Ojai in the fall and spring are fewer in number each year. I used to listen for the resonant honk of the Canadian geese, but they rarely pass over Ojai anymore. And where are the monarch butterflies landing these days? The bright orange clouds of monarchs that used to bring wild joy to me when I lived in Big Sur were smaller this year. I remember the flowering eucalyptus tree that hummed with the beating wings of these delicate creatures. In the heat of Ojai's summer nights, listening to the crickets' high-pitched song, I often thought of the impoverishment of being born and dying in New York or Mexico City, where these songs are not heard.

Sometimes it was difficult not to feel discouraged by the increasing noise of traffic on Highway 150, which ran beneath the ridge on which I lived, or the increased presence of airplanes on Sundays that flew over Ojai to view the valley below. Fasting in the desert near Death Valley, walking in the Sangre de Cristo Mountains every afternoon, military planes pass overhead as they train for a war that should not happen. I can no longer deny the consequences of living in a world where the humming of machines, not crickets, forms the auditory background of our dreams.

But airplanes and automobiles are part of my world too. Indeed, one of the ways I connect with the world around me is by traveling. I also connect with the world through words. There is no doubt in my mind that not a little has been sacrificed that these words can be read in this form. How shall I count the trees? My practice calls me not to forget or deny the outcome of the choices I have made about how I live. Looking deeply into the nature of these choices, that simply by living we take life, can open the heart of compassion as we feel the tread of our presence on the Earth. The Japanese call this "the slender sadness," *mono no aware.*

Some years ago at a Buddhist retreat for artists at the Ojai Foundation, we arrived under the oak tree to meditate and discovered that there was an arrangement of compost on the altar. Here were banana peels, egg shells, wood chips, and bits of dinner from the evening before. Someone asked Thich Nhat Hanh if this was disrespectful. He smiled and said, on the contrary, the arrangement was made by someone who truly understood the dharma.

In the Vietnamese form of Buddhism, there are small poems of mindfulness that can be recited to remind us of exactly what we are doing at this very moment. One of these *gathas* is for throwing out the garbage. It goes as follows:

In the garbage I see a rose.
In the rose, I see the garbage.
Everything is in transformation.
Even permanence is impermanent.

"Garbage can smell terrible," says Thich Nhat Hanh,

> especially rotting organic matter. But it can also become rich compost for fertilizing the garden. The fragrant rose and the stinking garbage are two sides of the same existence. Without one, the other cannot be. Everything is in transformation. The rose that wilts after six days will become a part of the garbage. After six months the garbage is transformed into a rose. When we speak of impermanence, we understand that everything is in transformation. This becomes that, and that becomes this.
>
> Looking deeply, we can contemplate one thing and see everything else in it. We are not disturbed by change when we see the interconnectedness and continuity of all things. It is not that the life of any individual is permanent, but that life itself continues. When we identify ourselves with life and go beyond the boundaries of a separate identity, we shall be able to see permanence in the impermanent, or the rose in the garbage.

In 1987, traveling back from Mount Kailas in western Tibet, I was delayed for several days when the old truck I was traveling in bogged down in the middle of the Brahmaputra River. I was exhausted and discouraged by the rigors of the travel. My Khampa truck companions were a rough group who exploited and fought with the local Drogpa nomads day after day. With little or nothing to eat, predawn departures, midnight encampments, and the abuse of riding in the crowded bed of this old Chinese beater, I was more than beginning to lose my enthusiasm for the high plateau of Tibet. So there we were, stuck in another river.

Not far from this scene was a group of small, ragged yak-hair tents inhabited by very old women who had long outlived their men. They had a few animals for milk and butter but little else. Seeing a solitary crone standing in an endless, bare landscape with cobalt skies hanging overhead filled me with a kind of wonder, and even fear.

On the third day of our involuntary visit to this impermanent settlement, my traveling companion unpacked our little cooking pot with great excitement, and we headed off to visit one of these bright old souls. There an old woman sat in her little smoky tent, her skin dark with years of sun combined with yak butter and dung smoke. Beside her was a bucket of the whitest yogurt I had ever seen. It was ours, she gestured, as much as we could take. She laughed as she refused my money. What good would this money do her out here?

I found it difficult to accept this gift. Clearly I was hungry, but didn't she need something in return? I was stunned and humbled. It seemed as if one of the old, dark hands of Kanzeon was ladling out nectar for all hungry beings of the three times and the four worlds.

When I look back on that moment by the river, I still can see those old female eyes burning with love. This fire is no different from the one I have seen in the eyes of Ogobara, Chan K'in Viejo, Guadalupe de la Cruz Ríos, Don José, and Maria Sabina. These old known and unknown men and women of elder cultures reside in the undifferentiated body of no-cause. This body is a wildfire and a lamp; it clears the brush and shows the way.

It is said that as we are dying, the last sense faculty to cease to function is our hearing. It is also said that things originally came into being through their vibration, through their sounding. "In the beginning was the Word," so the scriptures say. When a thing ceases to be, its sound disappears from the world. Kanzeon is the intimate presence of compassionate intelligence within all things that responds through perceiving the sound of life activity, no matter how small the voice, no matter how deep the suffering, how great the joy. I believe that Buddhism, shamanism, and deep ecology in their different ways are calling us to put our ear against the body of the Earth, to listen closely to what is really being said, and to consider the consequences of what we are hearing.

Breath, wind, and the holy Word are related through the experience of Spirit, the atmosphere of our World Psyche. Yet the atmosphere circulating through us is so polluted that hearing into, listening to, the Spirit of all things, into the World Psyche, though difficult, is a necessity for our common survival. Peoples of elder cultures often say that the survival of human beings depends on being able to hear the language of the birds and beasts, the language of the river, rock, and wind, being able to understand what is being said in all the tongues of plant, creature, and element. Listening to the garbage as well as the rose with the same ears, the ears of compassionate understanding. Who listens in this manner is Kanzeon. It is she who "abides in ultimate closeness" with all beings. It is she who embodies the principles of intimacy, simple communion, warmth, and mercy within each of us.

Do not say that I'll depart tomorrow
because even today I still arrive.

Look deeply; I arrive in every second
to be a bud on a spring branch,
to be a tiny bird, whose wings are still
    fragile, learning to sing in my new nest,
to be a caterpillar in the heart of a flower,
to be a jewel hiding itself in a stone.

I still arrive, in order to laugh and to cry, in
    order to fear and to hope,
the rhythm of my heart is the birth and
    death of all that are alive.

                        Thich Nhat Hanh

Epilogue

Earth brings us into life
and nourishes us.
Earth takes us back again.
Birth and death are present in every moment.
>   Thich Nhat Hanh

In the early eighties I, with others, walked along a Pacific beach late one afternoon on our way to an intertidal wilderness area some miles south. It was at dusk that we found a stranded dolphin not far from shore. Her skin was dry and printed raw with the pattern of a gill net. She was barely breathing and seemed to shrink in size as we approached her. The women in our party began to move her back into the surf. But again she stranded. Again we moved her, and this time her full weight, caught in a wave, injured the leg of one of the women. By this time it was dark, and so the dolphin rested on shore while we passed the night keeping her skin wet with seawater and breathing with her.

Early the next morning I hiked back to a nearby sand company, which let me use their phone to call all over California for help. I felt quite desperate. We did not know what to do with this dying creature and could not just leave her. So I decided to ask the "professionals" what to do. They had no answers either, or were too busy, or said, "Well, dolphins are stranding now."

On my way out of the sand company's office, I saw a stretcher leaning against the wall and also noticed that the giant front-loader, two stories tall and used to move sand, was the right size for dolphin and stretcher. Returning to the dolphin, I rode in the huge shovel of the front-loader.

From on high in this steel machine, I looked down on the dying dolphin and a meditating woman by her side. The contrast between the machine and the dying flesh was painful to behold. As I was being lowered to the sand, I was wrenched by a strong spasm of doubt. Enough of the heroism, I thought. But we did it anyway. We moved the dolphin from her sandy bed to a nearby aquarium where she died a short time later.

The following week we came upon a dying seal as we were walking along that same beach on our way north. The dolphin's suffering, which had deepened with our interference, was still with us. We remembered her exhausted eyes as she was hoisted onto the stretcher. We approached the seal, sat quietly nearby, and then left. That day I learned that sometimes the practice of nonviolence, of harmlessness, of harmony, means doing nothing or very little.

In *A Sand County Almanac,* Aldo Leopold expressed his sense that the human being is a "plain citizen" of the larger biotic community, neither more nor less. Biospecies equality; harmony with nature; recognition that Earth's so-called resources for the human being are limited, thereby requiring human commitment to a responsible relationship to our co-species and to an environment that supports all life on the planet; and a developed understanding of a global perspective as well as of our own particular bioregion—all these elements are at the core of the philosophy and practice of deep ecology. These perspectives are realized not just through the accumulation of scientific facts but through our direct experience with ourselves, one another, other species, and the environment we share. They are realized through an attitude of friendliness toward others and the craft of compassion, or appropriate action, the practice of harmlessness.

As in the story of the dolphin, we don't always know when to let go, when to abide in stillness. Indeed, loving-kindness is letting go and abiding in stillness. In Buddhism, loving-kindness is expressed by the Sanskrit term *maitri* and the Pali term *metta.* This word is derived from the term *mitta,* which means friend. Loving-kindness means then true friendliness, true friendliness to the reality of all things and all events—in their joy, in their suffering. This true friendliness toward Earth, this love and compassion for Earth, means freedom for Earth, and for ourselves. In Carlos Castaneda's *Tales of Power,* Don Juan says, "Only if one loves this earth with unending passion can one release one's sadness. A warrior is always joyful because his love is unalterable and his beloved, the earth, bestows upon him inconceivable gifts. . . . Only the love for this splendorous being can give freedom to a warrior's spirit; and freedom is joy, efficiency, and abandon in the face of any odds."

I know that those eyes that gaze with abandon into the world—this capacity for "seeing," for deeply understanding things as they are from within themselves—are the secret eyes of our true nature. They are the eyes that have looked into the fertile darkness. They are the "eyes of compassion." And this body, with its heart, hands, and feet is the greater vehicle for realizing loving-kindness—our feeling of oneness with oceans, forests, the great trees, and all creatures, this body born from darkness into light, this body that has traveled through a vast history from emptiness to form, this body in which identity is everywhere and nowhere.

> My whole body
> is covered with eyes:
> Behold it!
> Be without fear!
> I see all around.

This is the gift of the fruitful darkness, that we can see into the depths of suffering, our own and that of others, and in seeing, in understanding, we harvest the fruits of compassion. Thich Nhat Hanh once said, "Suffering is not enough." If we look deeply into ourselves we can see that our basic nature is free of suffering, that our lives fundamentally are wholesome and complete.

In Buddhism, our true nature is described in terms of "The Six Perfections," qualities that are intrinsic to each of us. These qualities are what we are at our core. When I extend my thinking to include greater nature, I see that the Perfections apply to the whole of creation as well as to the human part. They are true of wilderness. They are true of the stars and true of the empty sky. That is why for generations people have gone to the wilds to find and see their Perfection, their true nature, their inherent goodness, wholesomeness, and simplicity. We also go to the wilderness to see the Perfection of the extended body of creation of which we are a part. These qualities, intrinsic to our very being, are an expression of our enlightenment. Each quality is connected to all the others, making a net of interrelated conditions that express our awakened mind extending through the phenomenal world, a mind that is grounded in the perfection of emptiness.

Although in the Christian tradition, the term *perfection* is used to refer to the realization of wholeness, I usually prefer not to use the word *Perfection*. Perfection seems a bit daunting. In its place, I often use the terms *Inherent, Complete,* or *Natural* Condition.

The first Natural Condition is Generosity. If we look at nature as a whole, for example, it is, if nothing else, not selfish. Earth indeed is abundant if left to its own devices. Earth's abundance, its natural generosity, can cease when humans inter-fere with the alchemy of living forces. We are part of nature and are called to live in harmony with it. Living in balance with creation, we are in a con-tinuous state of generosity. In tribal cultures, this is expressed in the acts of purifying, sacrificing, and blessing—all strategies that emphasize empti-ness and interconnectedness. In Buddhism, we "practice" generosity in order to give assent to the quality of emptiness in ourselves and to the fact of our kinship to all beings, to all creation. And just as Earth takes care of itself, we can be inspired not only to practice generosity with others but also to take care of ourselves as well.

This is the first Natural or Inherent Condition, the "First Perfection." Being the first, it is impor-tant, for it sets the tone for the five that follow. In effect, all other conditions are born from generos-ity. And, interestingly, the root of the word *gen-erosity* is the same as that for the words *born* and *kin*. We express our enlightenment in terms of the affirmation of our relatedness to creation through our natural generosity. We can learn about our natural generosity from Earth.

The second Inherent Condition is Whole-someness. It is difficult for me to conceive of Earth as being unwholesome. In fact, even the savage as-pects of untamed nature feel clean and unsullied. When I see a viper in the rain forest, I don't feel that this one is unwholesome. Potentially danger-ous it is to me, yes, but certainly this viper has nat-ural virtue. When I spend time in an old growth cedar forest in the northwestern United States and look at the cycle of life reflected in standing cedar and the fallen and rotting bodies of old trees, I never feel as if this feeding of life with death is unwholesome. Yet human beings have often projected their alienation on nature in profoundly destructive ways and experienced the wilderness as corrupt. The wilderness is hardly corrupt, and we ourselves are called to return there to retrieve our natural wholesomeness.

In Buddhism, this Perfection is associated with the ten virtues of nonharming with body, speech, and mind. These virtues and the precepts or vows that we take in Buddhism are ways that we protect ourselves and others from suffering. In the Appendix, I have reproduced the Precepts of the Tiep Hien Order. I think that they can be quite helpful as a guide for mindful living. Indeed, we would not have to bother with precepts at all if we were truly aware. But, alas, most of us tend to forget. We don't see how and who we really are. So the Precepts remind us, just as the teachings on our natural wholesomeness remind us.

At our core, we are free from desire, hatred, and ignorance. The secretions of our minds, the accretions of the various forms of alienation that are part of our human condition, are what we work with in order for us to develop compassion. In fact, we need suffering in order to develop our ideal of compassion, for compassion arises from the darkness of human travail. It is the gift of our humanness, not to be denied but rather to be affirmed, to be sponsored, to be thoroughly understood.

The third Inherent Condition is Patience, Natural Patience or Transcendent Endurance. The wilderness teaches us patience with its unfolding in the long body of geological time. Trees teach us patience in their rootedness in the present moment, as do the migrating geese who fly on the fine edge of the seasons. Patience is about being in the present moment. It confirms each thing, each being, in its own terms. It is free of anger. It is release from hope and fear. It is acceptance of things exactly as they are. In this natural patience, in accepting things as they are, we are able to see deeply and to understand, to practice nondenial, and in this way to cultivate pure awareness.

Yes, natural patience is based in the unbiased mindstream, the uncorrected mind. I believe that the third line is the most important in this Zen *gatha* from Thich Nhat Hanh:

Breathing in, I calm body and mind.
Breathing out, I smile.
Dwelling in the present moment
This is the only moment.

The fourth Condition inherent to us and to greater nature is that of Energy, Natural Energy. Years ago, when I brought Don José to New York City, he told me that the energy in New York was not real energy, not the *kupuri* or "life energy force" of his world. He informed me that this stuff in New York would enslave and kill people, whereas *kupuri* freed them. This "life energy force" is found in sacred places, in waterfalls, ancestral rocks, in peyote and deer, in corn. When he went out to a restaurant in New York to have some steak, the old shaman refused to eat it, saying that it was dead, long dead. "No *kupuri*," he said.

Like the Huichols who go to the Zacatecan desert to renew their energy, to find their lives, we can go to the wilderness to reawaken this life energy force within us. The best that some of us can do is to get to Central Park or Hyde Park, to the beaches of New Jersey or Brighton, but we must turn away from the purely civilized in order to restore ourselves, to reawaken our intrinsic energy.

Sometimes this quality is referred to as "enthusiasm." It implies a psychophysical quality that engages us with practice, with the world, with each other. The word *enthusiasm* means "the god within." For me, it refers to a sense of shared divinity that pervades all creation. It is this energy body that ties the universe together, that dances, makes love, sings, laughs, and cries through us. It is the energy of sorrow and wrath, the energy of fear and aggression. Without our intrinsic energy, we cannot live. Nor can we transform or be transformed by the conditions within and around us.

The Inherent Condition following Energy is the experience of *samadhi* or Natural Concentration. Concentration, or the mind that holds still for change, is the mind of communion. It is a mind that abides in the true nature of each moment, each activity, each relationship that informs it. This mind is not divided from the body, nor is it separate from the greater body of nature. It abides in *samadhi,* in communion with all things, and all things abide in *samadhi* with it. The cottonwoods outside my window practice natural concentration. The crows and bald eagles who rest in their branches join the trees in collective *samadhi*. So also does the winter sun that melts the morning frost. And we too are in this web of communion, this net of concentration that is the continuum of creation. We can see it in the unstudied arrangement of the stars and galaxies. We catch a glimpse of it in the fine meander of a river, in the turning of old stone in the canyon's wall, in the Dakini-shaped cloud. From our *samadhi*, *vajras* (symbols of the Buddha-mind) spontaneously arise from boulders, the footprints of Padmasambhava can be found impressed on the floors of Himalayan caves, and a goddess's face appears in the ice of a high mountain lake. Communion is the ground of the ordinary and the miraculous. Wine and blood, bread and flesh. There are no boundaries in *samadhi*.

The sixth Inherent Condition is Wisdom, Natural Wisdom, the mind that is clear like a mirror, like space. Wisdom is the mother of generosity, wholesomeness, patience, energy, and concentration. These qualities cook within the belly of wisdom. I go to the wilderness to find the activity of natural wisdom. There I have discovered the roots of wisdom in the uncontrived and unstudied growth of green plants in the tropical forests, the boiling of clouds over southern islands, the deep skies embracing mountaintops, and the crow riding in the wind. Everywhere in these worlds I find a ready mind, not stopped by conceptual knowledge, the mind that does not have to stumble over strategy as it responds directly to the world. There is no strategy in the wilderness. It is a place where Truth is experienced and expressed directly.

Thus it is with the Six Natural Conditions that are the display of our true nature, our inherent enlightenment. Generosity, Wholesomeness, Patience, Enthusiasm, Communion, and Wisdom— all interconnected—are found in the ground of the fruitful darkness. This fertile darkness is where mystery lives, the great cloud of unknowing. Like the darkness of the fecund Earth that feeds corn and crow, the dark face of the goddess, of the wilderness, of our psyches, this deep ground feeds what we can call "our soul," that principle of communication that links the three times and four worlds. This is the connective element abiding in the interworld. What shines through "the eyes of compassion" is the principle of soul, that which has gone "down and in." The yield of the journey is expressed by the light pouring out of the windows of our interior worlds, the deep ground of our actual lives.

Abiquiu, New Mexico
Epiphany
January 6, 1992

Revolutionary Letter #68
Life Chant

may it come that all the radiances
will be known as our own radiance
                    Tibetan Book of the Dead

cacophony of small birds at dawn
    may it continue
sticky monkey flowers on bare brown hills
    may in continue
bitter taste of early miner's lettuce
    may it continue
music on city streets in the summer nights
    may it continue
kids laughing on roofs on stoops on the beach
    in the snow
    may it continue
triumphal shout of the newborn
    may it continue
deep silence of great rainforests
    may it continue
fine austerity of jungle peoples
    may it continue
rolling fuck of great whales in turquoise ocean
    may it continue
clumsy splash of pelican in smooth bays
    may it continue
astonished human eyeball squinting thru
    aeons at astonished
nebulae who squint back
    may it continue
clean snow on the mountain

may it continue
fierce eyes, clear light of the aged
    may it continue
rite of birth & naming
    may it continue
rite of instruction
    may it continue
rite of passage
    may it continue
love in the morning, love in the noon sun
love in the evening among crickets
    may it continue
long tales by fire, by window, in fog, in dusk
    on the mesa
    may it continue
love in thick midnight, fierce joy of old ones
    loving
    may it continue
the night music
    may it continue
grunt of mating hippo, giraffe, foreplay of
    snow leopard
screeching of cats on the backyard fence
    may it continue
without police
    may it continue
without prisons
    may it continue
without hospitals, death medicine: flu & flu
    vaccine
    may it continue
without madhouses, marriage, high schools
    that are prisons
    may it continue

without empire
    may it continue
in sisterhood
    may it continue
thru the wars to come
    may it continue
in brotherhood
    may it continue
tho the earth seem lost
    may it continue
thru exile & silence
    may it continue
with cunning and love
    may it continue
as woman continues
    may it continue
as breath continues
    may it continue
as stars continue
    may it continue
may the wind deal kindly w/ us
may the fire remember our names
many springs flow, rain fall again
may the land grown green, may it swallow
    our mistakes
we begin the work
    may it continue
the great transmutation
    may it continue
a new heaven & a new earth
    may it continue
    may it continue

                    Diane di Prima

Appendix

Precepts of the Order of Interbeing

The First Precept: Do not be idolatrous about or bound to any doctrine, theory, or ideology, even Buddhist ones. All systems of thought are guiding means; they are not absolute truth.

The Second Precept: Do not think that the knowledge you presently possess is changeless, absolute truth. Avoid being narrow-minded and bound to present views. Learn and practice nonattachment from views in order to be open to receive others' viewpoints. Truth is found in life and not merely in conceptual knowledge. Be ready to learn throughout your entire life and to observe reality in yourself and in the world at all times.

The Third Precept: Do not force others, including children, by any means whatsoever, to adopt your views, whether by authority, threat, money, propaganda, or even education. However, through compassionate dialogue, help others renounce fanaticism and narrowness.

The Fourth Precept: Do not avoid contact with suffering or close your eyes before suffering. Do not lose awareness of the existence of suffering in the life of the world. Find ways to be with those who are suffering by all means, including personal contact and visits, images, sounds. By such means awaken yourself and others to the reality of suffering in the world.

The Fifth Precept: Do not accumulate wealth

while millions are hungry. Do not take as the aim of your life fame, profit, wealth, or sensual pleasure. Live simply and share time, energy, and material resources with those who are in need.

The Sixth Precept: Do not maintain anger or hatred. Learn to penetrate and transform them when they are still seeds in your consciousness. As soon as they arise, turn your attention to your breath in order to see and understand the nature of your anger and hatred and the nature of the persons who have caused your anger and hatred.

The Seventh Precept: Do not lose yourself in dispersion and in your surroundings. Practice mindful breathing to come back to what is happening in the present moment. Be in touch with what is wondrous, refreshing, and healing both inside and around you. Plant seeds of joy, peace, and understanding in yourself in order to facilitate the work of transformation in the depths of your consciousness.

The Eighth Precept: Do not utter words that can create discord and cause the community to break. Make every effort to reconcile and resolve all conflicts, however small.

The Ninth Precept: Do not say untruthful things for the sake of personal interest or to impress people. Do not utter words that cause division and hatred. Do not spread news that you do not know to be certain. Do not criticize or condemn things that you are not sure of. Always speak truthfully and constructively. Have the courage to speak out about situations of injustice, even when doing so may threaten your own safety.

The Tenth Precept: Do not use the Buddhist community for personal gain or profit, or transform your community into a political party. A religious community, however, should take a clear stand against oppression and injustice and should strive to change the situation without engaging in partisan conflicts.

The Eleventh Precept: Do not live with a vocation that is harmful to humans and nature. Do not invest in companies that deprive others of their chance to live. Select a vocation that helps realize your ideal of compassion.

The Twelfth Precept: Do not kill. Do not let others kill. Find whatever means possible to protect life and prevent war.

The Thirteenth Precept: Possess nothing that should belong to others. Respect the property of others, but prevent others from enriching themselves from human suffering or the suffering of other species on Earth.

The Fourteenth Precept: Do not mistreat your body. Learn to handle it with respect. Do not look on your body as only an instrument. Preserve vital energies (sexual, breath, spirit) for the realization of the Way. Sexual expression should not take place without love and a long-term commitment. In sexual relationships be aware of future suffering that may be caused. To preserve the happiness of others, respect the rights and commitments of others. Be fully aware of the responsibility of bringing new lives into the world. Meditate on the world into which you are bringing new beings.

Notes

Preface

xix What the people . . . .: Chan K'in Viejo in Victor
Perera and Robert Bruce, *The Last Lords of Palenque*
(Berkeley: Univ. of California Press, 1985), 86.

Chapter One: The World Wound

6 Here on this mountain . . .: Nancy Wood, *War Cry
on a Prayer Feather* (Garden City, NY: Doubleday,
1979), 107.

17 and press their . . . .: Wendell Berry, *The Long-Legged
House* (New York: Harcourt Brace and World,
1969), 41.

19 The first step . . .: Marie-Louise von Franz, *The
Feminine in Fairy Tales* (Dallas: Spring Publications,
1972), 64.

Chapter Two: The Way of Silence

25 The wicasa wakan . . .: John Fire Lame Deer and
Richard Erdoes, *Lame Deer: Seeker of Visions* (New
York: Simon and Schuster, 1972), 155–56.

26 climbed the blue . . . .: from *Shaking the Pumpkin,*
trans. Jerome Rothenberg (New York: Doubleday,
1972), 363.

26 Our eyes remain . . .: García Lorca. I regret that I've
been unable to locate a published source for these
lines from a Lorca poem.

27 All is seared . . .: Gerard Manley Hopkins, "God's
Grandeur," *Poems of Gerard Manley Hopkins* (New
York: Oxford Univ. Press, 1948), 70.

28 In our bones . . . .: Nancy Wood, *War Cry on a
Prayer Feather* (Garden City, NY: Doubleday,
1979), 12.

28 When I was to be an anatkoq . . .: *The Intellectual
Culture of Caribou Eskimos* 7:2 (Copenhagen:
Report of the 5th Thule Expedition, 1930), 51.

29   Fast and pray . . .: *The Essene Gospel of Peace,* trans.
      Edmond B. Szekely (San Diego: Academy of
      Creative Living, 1971), 15.

Chapter Three: The Way of Traditions

39   Our symbols, the deer . . .: Ramón Medina Silva in
      Barbara Myerhoff, *Peyote Hunt* (Ithaca, NY: Cornell
      Univ. Press, 1974), 264.

45   Look you *tevainuríxi* . . .: Peter Furst and Marina
      Anguiano, "'To Fly as Birds': Myth and Ritual as
      Agents of Enculturation among the Huichol
      Indians of Mexico,'" in *Enculturation in Latin
      America: An Anthology,* ed. Johannes Wilbert (Los
      Angeles: UCLA Latin American Center
      Publications, 1976), 150–51.

Chapter Four: The Way of the Mountain

54   Inexhaustible is their . . .: Michael Tobias, "A
      History of Imagination in Wilderness," in *The
      Mountain Spirit,* ed. Michael Tobias and Harold
      Drasdo (Woodstock: The Overlook Press, 1979),
      208.

55   I climb the . . .: Han-shan in *Cold Mountain,* trans.
      Burton Watson (New York: Columbia Univ. Press,
      1970), 58.

56   The sound of . . .: from *The Blue Cliff Records,* vol.
      II, trans. Thomas and J. C. Chenery (Boulder:
      Shambhala, 1977), 277.

56   Mountains and rivers . . .: adapted by the author
      from two translations of Eihei Dōgen, "Mountains
      and Rivers Sutra": *Moon in a Dewdrop,* ed. Kazuaki
      Tanahashi (San Francisco: North Point Press, 1985),
      97–107 and "Dōgen's Shobogenzo Snsuikyo" by
      Carl Bielefeldt in *The Mountain Spirit,* ed. Michael
      Tobias and Harold Drasdo (Woodstock: The
      Overlook Press, 1979), 37–50.

57   The blue mountains . . .: ibid, 57–58

73   The birds have . . .: Li Po, trans. Sam Hamill, *The
      Enlightened Heart,* ed. Stephen Mitchell (New York:
      Harper & Row, 1989), 32.

74 One summer a few years ago . . .: Alfonso Ortiz,
    "Look to the Mountaintop," *Essays on Relections II,*
    ed. E. Graham Ward (Boston: Houghton Mifflin,
    1973), 89–90.

76 these [sacred] mountains . . .: Gladys Reichard,
    Navaho Religion, Bollingen Series XVIII (Princeton:
    Princeton Univ. Press, 1974), 19–20.

77 Within and around . . .: Alfonso Ortiz, *The Tewa
    World* (Chicago: Univ. of Chicago Press, 1969), 13.

Chapter Five: The Way of Language

83 Earth / Sky / Mountain Woman . . .: Gladys
    Reichard, *Navaho Religion,* Bollingen Series XVIII
    (Princeton: Princeton Univ. Press, 1974), 273.

83 The one called Holy . . .: J. K. McNeley, *Holy Wind
    in Navajo Philosophy* (Tucson: Univ. of Arizona
    Press, 1981), 35.

85 Old jay, loudmouth . . .: Howard Norman, *Wishing
    Bone Cycle* (Santa Barbara: Ross-Erikson
    Publishing, 1982), 103.

87 heya heya heya . . .: Fr. Berard Haile, *Origin
    Legends of the Navajo Enemy Way* (New Haven: Yale
    Univ. Publications in Anthropology, no. 17, 1938),
    265.

89 I'm the mad . . .: Vicente Huidobro, "Altazor," in
    The Selected Poetry of Vicente Huidobro, ed. David
    Guss (New York: New Directions, 1981).

89 The fish does . . .: trans. C. M. Bowra in *Primitive
    Song* (Cleveland: World Publishing Co., 1962),
    106.

91 Sometimes, when a bird . . .: Hermann Hesse in
    News from the Universe, trans. Robert Bly (San
    Francisco: Sierra Club Books, 1980), 86.

98 long ago brown bears . . .: William Oandasan, from
    Round Valley Songs (Minneapolis: West End Press,
    1984), 23.

Chapter Six: The Way of Story

104   My father went on talking . . .: Ruth Underhill, *Autobiography of a Papago Woman,* Memoirs of the AAA, no. 46 (Menasha, WI: Kraus Reprint Co., 1974, 1936), 36.

112   It was foretold . . .: Grandfather David Monongye from a transcription given to the author by Joan Price.

114   We always pray . . .: Leon Shenandoah, from a talk given at Crestone, Colorado, 1991 and from *Wisdomkeepers* (Hillsboro, OR: Beyond Words Publishing, 1990), 102–8.

115   Eat, eat, thou hast bread . . .: Daniel G. Brinton, *The Maya Chronicles* (Library of Aboriginal American Literature Series #1; New York: AMS Press, 1982, 1970), 127.

117   We are poor . . .: Anna Benson Gyles and Chloe Sayer, *Of Gods and Men* (New York: Harper & Row, 1980), 170.

121   I live, but . . .: Willard Rhodes, "Indian Songs of Today," unpaged typescript to be published as a booklet accompanying Library of Congress Phonograph Album AFS-L-36, Washington, DC: Library of Congress Folk Archives.

122   This instrument was not . . .: *Popol Vuh: The Mayan Book of the Dawn of Life,* trans. Dennis Tedlock (New York: Touchstone Books, Simon & Schuster, 1985), 23.

123   The day has risen, . . .: H. R. Voth (Chicago: Field Museum of Natural History Anthropological Publications, vol. 6, no.1, 1903), 39.

124   i speak for . . .: Hans Magnus Enzensberger, "The End of the Owls," from *New Young German Poets,* ed. Jerome Rothenberg (San Francisco: City Lights, 1959), 62.

124   The Crow / I . . .: James Mooney, "The Ghost Dance Religion," Bureau of American Ethnology 14th Annual Report, 1892–92, pt. 2, 1035.

Chapter Seven: The Way of Nonduality

130 In the dark times . . .: Bertolt Brecht. I regret that
     I found these lines in a book that did not cite their
     source.

133 Why do we adore . . .: Ramón Medina Silva in
     Barbara Myerhoff, *Peyote Hunt* (Ithaca: Cornell
     Univ. Press, 1974), 78–79.

137 All is a circle . . .: Nancy Wood, *War Cry on a
     Prayer Feather* (Garden City, NY: Doubleday,
     1979), 105, and in the forthcoming *Spirit Walker*
     (New York: Doubleday Books for Young Readers,
     1993).

139 You should entreat . . .: Eihei Dōgen, "Paying
     Homage and Acquiring the Essence," in Francis
     Dojun Cook, *How to Raise an Ox* (Los Angeles:
     Center Publications, 1978), 135.

140 Being an Indian . . .: Julian Berger, *The Gaia Atlas of
     First Peoples* (New York: Anchor Books, Doubleday,
     1990), 16.

140 Because I spent . . .: Nancy Wood, *War Cry on a
     Prayer Feather* (Garden City, NY: Doubleday,
     1979), 79.

141 Heaven is my father . . .: Chang-tsai in Thomas
     Berry, *The Dream of the Earth* (San Francisco: Sierra
     Club Books, 1990), 14.

142 Oh Olelbes, look . . .: Sadie Marsh in Dorothy D.
     Lee, "Some Indian Texts Dealing with the
     Supernatural," in *Review of Religion,* vol. 5, 1941,
     407.

144 We do not like . . .: William Jones, *Ethnography of
     the Fox Indians* (Washington, DC: BAEB 125,
     Government Printing Office, 1939).

144 Johannes Wilbert, "To Become a Maker of Canoes:
     An Essay on Warao Enculturation," in *Enculturation
     in Latin America: An Anthology,* ed. Johannes
     Wilbert (Los Angeles: UCLA Latin American
     Center Publications, 1976), 341.

145   Werner Wilbert wrote on the Warao in "The
      Pneumatic Theory of Female Warao Herbalists,"
      Soc. Sci. Med., vol. 25, no. 10, Great Britain, 1987,
      1139–46.

148   With this holy pipe . . .: John Fire Lame Deer and
      Richard Erdoes, *Lame Deer: Seeker of Visions* (New
      York: Simon & Schuster, 1972), 253.

149   All the Powers of the world . . .: Joseph Epes
      Brown, *The Sacred Pipe* (Norman: Univ. of
      Oklahoma Press, 1953), 47.

150   In the beginning . . .: Nancy Wood, *War Cry on a
      Prayer Feather* (Garden City, NY: Doubleday, 1979),
      14, and in the forthcoming *Spirit Walker* (New
      York: Doubleday Books for Young Readers, 1993).

151   While I stood there . . .: John G. Neihardt, *Black Elk
      Speaks* (Lincoln: Univ. of Nebraska Press, 1961),
      43.

151   In our bones . . .: Nancy Wood, *War Cry on a Prayer
      Feather* (Garden City, NY: Doubleday, 1979), 12.

152   At the edge . . .: Ruth Underhill, *Red Man's Religion*
      (Chicago: Univ. of Chicago Press, 1965), 245.

152   Ecological thinking . . .: Paul Shepard,
      "Introduction—Ecology of Man—a View Point," in
      *The Subversive Science: Essays Toward an Ecology of
      Man*, ed. Paul Shepard and Daniel McKinley
      (Boston: Houghton Mifflin, 1969), 2.

153   In this plate of food . . .: Thich Nhat Hanh in
      Dharma Gaia, ed. Allan Hunt-Badiner (Berkeley:
      Parallax Press, 1990), 195.

157   Soil for legs . . .: Nanao Sakaki, *Break the Mirror*
      (San Francisco: North Point Press, 1987), 89.

158   I entered the life . . .: Robinson Jeffers, "The Tower
      Beyond Tragedy," in *The Selected Poetry of Robinson
      Jeffers* (New York: Random House, 1938), 138–39.

160   A human being is . . .: Thich Nhat Hanh, "The
      Individual, Society, and Nature," *The Path of
      Compassion* (Berkeley: Parallax Press, 1988), 41.

161   I'm in it everywhere . . .: Ikkyu, trans. Stephen Berg in *Crow with No Mouth* (Port Townsend, WA: Copper Canyon Press, 1989).

161   It is said that insentient . . .: Zen Master Tung Shan, quoted in a lecture by Richard Baker Roshi.

162   We are Nature . . .: Walt Whitman, "We Two, How Long We Were Fooled," *Leaves of Grass* (New York: Random House, n.d.), 89.

163   Our old women gods . . .: H. J. Spinden, *Songs of the Tewa* (Santa Fe: Sunstone Press, 1976), 106.

Chapter Eight: The Way of Protectors

171   The temple of the animals . . .: Robert Duncan, *Selected Poems* (San Francisco: City Lights, 1959), 36.

Chapter Nine: The Way of the Ancestors

188   We reached the old . . .: Aldo Leopold, *A Sand County Almanac* (New York: Oxford University Press, 1949), 130.

189   But when I breathe . . .: Theodore Roethke, "Journey to the Interior," *The Far Field* (Garden City, NY: Doubleday, 1958), 21.

191   The mountain, I become . . .: Dineh chant from Peter Nabokov, *Indian Running* (Santa Fe: Ancient City Press, 1987), 193.

Chapter Ten: The Way of Compassion

198   How does the Bodhisattva . . .: *The Blue Cliff Records* from Nelson Foster, "To Enter the Marketplace," in *The Path of Compassion* (Berkeley: Parallax Press, 1988), 57–58.

199   When I was a kid . . .: Peggy Beck and Anna Walters, *The Sacred: Ways of Knowledge, Sources of Life* (Tsaile, AZ: The Navajo Community College Press, 1972), 23.

200   I feel for the sores . . .: Peter Knudtsen, "Flora: Shaman of the Wintu," *Natural History Magazine,* May 1975, 12.

200 Unless we see or hear . . .: Basho Matsuo in
Dharma Gaia, ed. Allan Hunt-Badiner (Berkeley:
Parallax Press, 1990), 191.

204 In the garbage . . .: Thich Nhat Hanh, *Present
Moment, Wonderful Moment: Mindfulness Verse for
Daily Living* (Berkeley: Parallax Press, 1990), 65.

205 Garbage can smell . . .: ibid, 65–66.

Epilogue

213 Only if one loves . . .: Carlos Castaneda, *Tales of
Power* (New York: Simon & Schuster, 1974),
285–86.

214 My whole body . . .: Edward Moffat Weyer, Jr., *The
Eskimos: Their Environment and Folkways* (New
Haven: Yale Univ. Press, 1932), 401.

218 Breathing in, I calm . . .: Thich Nhat Hanh from a
talk in Plum Village, 1986. Also published in
slightly modified form in *Being Peace* (Berkeley:
Parallax Press, 1988), 5.

This constitutes a continuation of the copyright page.

Grateful acknowledgment is made to the following for permission
to reprint material:

to Clarke Abbey for permission to reprint "Benedicto" by Edward
Abbey.

to AMS Press, Inc. for excerpt from *The Maya Chronicles*, edited by
Daniel G. Brinton (Library of Aboriginal American Literature
Series: #1; New York: AMS Press, 1970, 1882); for excerpt from
Songs of the Tewa, by H. J. Spinden (New York: Exposition of
Indian Tribal Arts, 1933) (AMS Press, reprint of 1933 edition).

to Robert Bly for excerpt from *Times Alone* by Antonio Machado,
translated by Robert Bly, copyright © 1982, Wesleyan
University Press.

to Carlos Castaneda for excerpt from *Tales of Power* by Carlos
Castaneda, copyright © 1974, Simon & Schuster Publishing.
Reprinted by permission of the author.

to Columbia University Press. Excerpt from *Cold Mountain*, by
Burton Watson, copyright © 1970, Columbia University Press,
New York. Reprinted with the permission of the publisher.

to Copper Canyon Press. Excerpt from *Crow with No Mouth: Ikkyu
15th Century Zen Master* copyright © 1989 by Stephen Berg.
Reprinted by permission of Copper Canyon Press, P.O. Box
271, Port Townsend, WA 98368.

to Cornell University Press for excerpts from *Peyote Hunt: The
Sacred Journey of Huichol Indians*, by Barbara Myerhoff, copyright © 1974 by Cornell University. Used by permission of the
publisher, Cornell University Press.

to Diane di Prima for "Revolutionary Letter #68: Life Chant" from
Revolutionary Letters Etc. (4th Ed.), City Lights Books, San
Francisco, copyright © 1979 by Diane di Prima.

to Doubleday & Company. Excerpt from *Gaia Atlas of First Peoples*
by Julian Berger, copyright © 1990; lines from "Journey to the
Interior," in *The Far Field* by Theodore Roethke, copyright ©
1958. Reprinted by permission of Doubleday & Co., a division
of Bantam Doubleday Dell Publishing Group, Inc.; for excerpts
from *Spirit Walker* by Nancy Wood, copyright © 1993 by
Nancy Wood, published by Doubleday Books for Young
Readers, a division of Bantam Doubleday Dell Publishing
Group, Inc.

to Farrar, Straus & Giroux, Inc. "Just Enough" from *Break The
Mirror*, copyright © 1987 by Nanao Sakaki. Published by North
Point Press and reprinted by permission of Farrar, Straus &
Giroux, Inc. Material adapted from "Shobogenzo Sansui-kyo,"
translated by Arnold Kotler and Kazuaki Tanahashi, in *Moon in
a Dewdrop: Writings of Zen Master Dōgen* edited by Kazuaki
Tanahashi, copyright © 1985, published by North Point Press;
for excerpt from "The Long-Legged House" from *Recollected
Esssays 1965–1980*, by Wendell Berry, copyright © 1969, 1981

237

by Wendell Berry. Published by North Point Press and reprinted by permission of Farrar, Straus & Giroux, Inc.

to HarperCollins Publishers. Excerpt from *Woman and Nature* by Susan Griffin. Copyright © 1978 by Susan Griffin. Excerpt from *The Enlightened Heart* translated by Stephen Mitchell. Copyright © 1989 by Stephen Mitchell. Excerpt from *Tao Te Ching* translated by Stephen Mitchell. Copyright © 1988 by Stephen Mitchell. Excerpts from *Of Gods and Men* by Anna Benson Gyles and Chloe Sayer. Copyright © 1980 by Anna Benson Gyles and Chloe Sayer. Excerpt from *Jambalaya* by Luisah Teish. Copyright © 1985 by Luisah Tiesh. Reprinted by permission of HarperCollins Publishers.

to Houghton Mifflin Company. Excerpt by Alfonso Ortiz from *Essays on Reflections II,* edited by E. Graham Ward, copyright © 1973, Houghton Mifflin Company.

to I.B.S. International. Excerpt from *The Essene Gospel of Peace,* translated by Edmund B. Szekeley, copyright © 1971, Academy of Creative Living. I.B.S. International, Matsqui, B.C., Canada.

to *Journal of Anthropological Research.* Excerpt quoted with permission from W. W. Hill, "Navaho Trading and Trading Ritual: A Study of Cultural Dynamics," *Southwestern Journal of Anthropology,* vol. 4, 1948, p. 384.

to Little, Brown & Company. Excerpt from *The Last Lords of Palenque,* by Victor Perera and Robert Bruce, copyright © 1985, Little, Brown & Company.

to *Natural History.* Excerpt from Peter Knudtsen, "Flora: Shaman of the Wintu"; with permission from *Natural History,* May, 1975; copyright © The American Museum of Natural History, 1975.

to the Navajo Community College Press. Excerpt from *The Sacred: Ways of Knowledge,* by Peggy Beck and Anna Walters. Copyright © The Navajo Community College Press.

to New Directions Publishing Corp. "Altazor," from Vicente Huidobro: *Selected Poetry of Vicente Huidobro.* Copyright © 1981 by New Directions Publishing Corporation. Reprinted by permission of New Directions Publishing Corp.

to New Society Publishers. "Spirit of Love" from *We Are All Part of One Another: A Barbara Deming Reader,* edited by Jane Meyerding, copyright © 1984. Reprinted by permission from New Society Publishers, 4527 Springfield Avenue, Philadelphia, PA 19143, 1-800-333-9093.

to William Oandasan. Excerpt from "Round Valley Songs" by William Oandasan, in *Round Valley Songs,* copyright © 1984, West End Press.

to Oxford University Press, Inc. Excerpt from *A Sand County Almanac* and *Sketches Here and There,* by Aldo Leopold. Copyright © 1949, 1977, by Oxford University Press, Inc. Reprinted by premission.

to Overlook Press. Excerpt from "A History of Imagination in Wilderness" by Kuo Hsi in *The Mountain Spirit* edited by Michael Tobias and Harold Drasdo. Copyright © 1979 by Michael Tobias and Harold Drasdo. Translated by Michael Tobias. Published by the Overlook Press, Woodstock, NY 12498. Excerpt and material adapted from "The Mountains and Rivers

Sutra" by Dōgen in *The Mountain Spirit* edited by Michael Tobias and Harold Drasdo. Copyright © 1979 by Michael Tobias and Harold Drasdo. Translated by Carl Bielefeldt. Published by the Overlook Press, Woodstock, NY 12498. Reprinted by permission of the Overlook Press and Carl Bielefeldt.

to Parallax Press. Excerpts reprinted by permission from *Dharma Gaia: A Harvest of Essays in Buddhism and Ecology* edited by Allan Hunt-Badiner, Parallax Press, Berkeley, California, 1990; excerpts reprinted by permission from *The Path of Compassion* edited by Fred Eppsteiner, Parallax Press, Berkeley, California, 1988; excerpts reprinted by permission from *Present Moment, Wonderful Moment* by Thich Nhat Hanh, Parallax Press, Berkeley, California, 1990; excerpts reprinted by permission from *Being Peace* by Thich Nhat Hanh, Parallax Press, Berkeley, California, 1987.

to Princeton University Press. Excerpts from *Navaho Religion* by Gladys Reichard, Bollingen Series XVIII; copyright © 1974, Princeton University Press.

to Random House, Inc. From *The Selected Poetry of Robinson Jeffers* by Robinson Jeffers. Copyright 1925 and renewed 1953 by Robinson Jeffers. Reprinted by permission of Random House, Inc.

to Ross-Erikson Publishing. Lines from *Wishing Bone Cycle* by Howard Norman, copyright © 1982. Ross-Erikson Publishing.

to Jerome Rothenberg for permission to quote from *Shaking the Pumpkin*, translated by Jerome Rothenberg, copyright © 1972, Doubleday & Company Publishers, and from *New Young German Poets* edited by Jerome Rothenberg, copyright © 1959, City Lights Books.

to Shambhala Publications, Inc. Excerpt from *The Feminine in Fairy Tales*, by Marie-Louise von Franz, copyright © 1972. Reprinted by arrangement with Shambhala Publications, Inc., 300 Massachusetts Ave., Boston, MA 02115.

to Paul Shepard. Excerpt from "Introduction—Ecology and Man— a View Point," by Paul Shepard, in *The Subversive Science: Essays Toward an Ecology of Man,* edited by Paul Shepard and Daniel McKinley (Boston: Houghton Mifflin, 1969).

to Sierra Club Books. "Oceans," by Juan Ramón Jiménez, translated by Robert Bly from *News of the the Universe,* by Robert Bly. Copyright © 1980 by Robert Bly. "Sometimes," by Hermann Hesse, translated by Robert Bly from *News of the Universe,* by Robert Bly. Copyright © 1980 by Robert Bly. Reprinted with permission of Sierra Club Books. Excerpt from *The Dream of the Earth* by Thomas Berry. Copyright © 1988 by Thomas Berry. Reprinted with permission of Sierra Club Books.

to Simon & Schuster, Inc. Excerpts from *Lame Deer: Seeker of Visions* by John Fire Lame Deer and Richard Erdoes, copyright © 1972, Simon & Schuster. Excerpt from *Popol Vuh,* trans. by Dennis Tedlock, copyright © 1985, Simon & Schuster, Inc. Reprinted by permission of Simon & Schuster, Inc.

to Sunstone Press for "Our old woman gods." This poem, courtesy of Sunstone Press (Box 2321, Santa Fe, NM 87504), is from *Songs of the Tewa* by H. J. Spinden.

to Threshold Books. Excerpt from *Open Secret,* translated by John Moyne and Coleman Barks; excerpt from *Unseen Rain: Quatrains of Rumi,* translated by John Moyne and Coleman Barks. Threshold Books, RD 4, Box 600, Putney, VT 05346.

to Tooth of Time Books. "Why," by Nanao Sakaki, *Real Play* (Santa Fe: Tooth of Time Books, 1981).

to University of Arizona Press. Excerpt from *Holy Wind In Navajo Philosophy* by James K. McNeley, copyright © 1981, University of Arizona Press.

to University of California at Los Angeles Latin American Center. Excerpts from Peter Furst and Marina Anguiano, "'To Fly As Birds': Myth and Ritual as Agents of Enculturation among the Huichol Indians of Mexico" and excerpt from Johannes Wilbert, "To Become a Maker of Canoes: An Essay in Warao Enculturation," in Johannes Wilbert, ed., *Enculturation in Latin America: An Anthology* (Los Angeles: UCLA Latin American Center Publications, 1976).

to University of Chicago Press. Excerpt from *The Tewa World: Space, Time, Being, and Becoming in a Pueblo Society* by Alfonso Ortiz, © 1969 by the University of Chicago, University of Chicago Press; excerpt from *Red Man's Religion: Beliefs and Practices of the Indians North of Mexico* by Ruth Underhill, © 1965 by the University of Chicago, University of Chicago Press.

to University of Nebraska Press. Excerpt reprinted from *Black Elk Speaks,* by John G. Neihardt, by permission of the University of Nebraska Press. Copyright © 1932, 1959, 1972, by John G. Neihardt. Copyright © 1961 by the John G. Neihardt Trust.

to University of Oklahoma Press. Excerpt from *The Sacred Pipe: Black Elk's Account of the Seven Rites of the Oglala Sioux,* by Joseph E. Brown. copyright © 1953 by the University of Oklahoma Press.

to Yale University Press. Excerpt from *Origin Legends of the Navajo Enemy Way* by Fr. Bernard Haile, copyright © 1938. Yale University Publications in Anthropology. Excerpt from *The Eskimos: Their Environment and Folkways* by E. M. Weyer, Jr., copyright © 1932, Yale University Press. Reprinted by permission of Yale University Press.

to Steve Wall and Harvey Arden, and to Beyond Words Publishing. For excerpts from *Wisdomkeepers: Meetings with Native American Spiritual Elders* by Steve Wall and Harvey Arden, copyright © 1990, Beyond Words Publishing.

to the Wheelwright Museum of the American Indian for permission to reprint an excerpt from the Mountain Chant.

to Nancy Wood for permission to use excerpts from *War Cry on a Prayer Feather,* published by Doubleday & Co., copyright © 1979 by Nancy Wood; and from *Spirit Walker,* published by Doubleday Books for Young Readers, a division of Bantam Doubleday Dell Publishing Group, Inc., copyright © 1993 by Nancy Wood. All rights reserved.

to Zen Center of Los Angeles. Excerpt from *How to Raise an Ox* by Francis Dojun Cook, copyright © 1978, Center Publications. Reprinted by permission of Zen Center of Los Angeles.

240